Somos así EN SUS MARCAS A

Second Edition

Workbook

Karin D. Fajardo
Peter M. Morales

Consultants
Amy Dorn-Fernández
James F. Funston
Yuri M. Guerra Guerra
Alejandro Vargas Bonilla

EMC/Paradigm Publishing, Saint Paul, Minnesota

The Internet is a fast-paced technology, and Web pages and Web addresses are constantly changing or disappearing. You may need to substitute different addresses from the ones given in the activities throughout this workbook.

ISBN 0-8219-1957-1

Published by EMC/Paradigm Publishing
875 Montreal Way
St. Paul, Minnesota 55102
800-328-1452
www.emcp.com
E-mail: educate@emcp.com

Printed in the United States of America
3 4 5 6 7 8 9 10 XXX 05 04 03 02 01

Nombre: ______________________ Fecha: ______________

CAPÍTULO 1

Lección 1

1 Los países de habla hispana

A. América Central, América del Norte y el Caribe

Write the names of the Spanish-speaking countries indicated by each number. Refer to the maps in the textbook of Central America, Mexico and the Caribbean.

Costa Rica	El Salvador	Honduras	Nicaragua	Puerto Rico
Cuba	Guatemala	México	Panamá	República Dominicana

1. ______________ 6. ______________

2. ______________ 7. ______________

3. ______________ 8. ______________

4. ______________ 9. ______________

5. ______________ 10. ______________

B. América del Sur, Europa y África

Complete each blank space with the names of the Spanish-speaking countries in South America, Europe and Africa.

Argentina	Colombia	Guinea Ecuatorial	Uruguay
Bolivia	Ecuador	Paraguay	Venezuela
Chile	España	Perú	

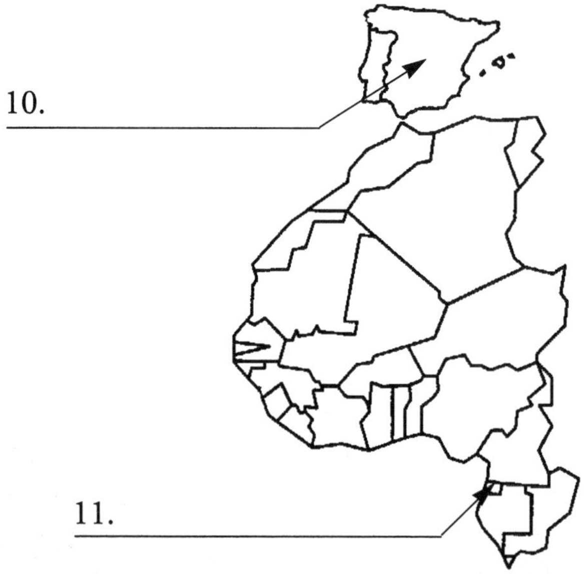

mbre: ______________________________ Fecha: ______________

Navegando por la red

You have logged on to the Internet to find information about Spanish-speaking countries and you have opened a page called *Oficinas de turismo* (Tourist Information Offices). A list of cities where these offices are located is displayed, but the countries are not listed. What buttons would you click to get information on each of the countries listed below the screen? In the space provided, write the letter for each city next to its corresponding country.

______ 1. Argentina

______ 2. El Salvador

______ 3. Colombia

______ 4. Cuba

______ 5. España

______ 6. Guatemala

______ 7. Nicaragua

______ 8. Paraguay

______ 9. Perú

______ 10. Venezuela

Nombre: ______________________ Fecha: ______________

3 Oportunidades: el español y tu futuro

Circle the occupations where Spanish might be needed.

4 Nombres

You are reading a Spanish-language magazine and you want to find out information about its editorial staff. Look at the listing below. Then read the statements that follow to determine which are true and which are false. Write **V** for *verdadero* (true) and **F** for *falso* (false) in the space provided.

Consejo Editorial/Presidente
Francisco Pérez de Antón
Vicepresidente
Fernando Quezada Toruño

Director
Haroldo Shetemul

Subdirectora
Evelyn Blanck

Jefe de Información
Félix Colindres

Economía: Carlos Morales Monzón
Internacional: César León
Cultura y Ocio: Silvia Lanuza
Actualidad: Roberto Samayoa Ochoa

Gerente General
Ana María Armand de Vizcaíno
Gerente de Publicidad
Carmen Urrutia de Aguilar
Gerente de Comercialización
Patricia Lehnhoff de Véliz

Separación de Portada
Crónica
Redacción y Administración
6a. Avenida, 0-60, Zona 4
Edificio Torre Profesional II,
Oficina 312, Guatemala, C.A.
Tels.: 3352155, 3351693,
3352351 y 3352355.
E-mail: Cronica@guate.net
FAX: 3352360 y 3352364

______ 1. There are as many men as women working for the magazine.

______ 2. The director is a woman.

______ 3. Seven male names appear in the list.

______ 4. Most people listed have two first names.

______ 5. Most people have two last names.

5 Correo electrónico

You had prepared a list of people you were planning to e-mail, but the word-processing application on your computer has scrambled the names. Unscramble the letters and write your friends' names in the space provided.

1. L A R I P ______________________
2. C T O V Í R ______________________
3. Q L E R A U ______________________
4. Z E P A S E A R N ______________________
5. A B N J E M N Í ______________________
6. C E E E S M R D ______________________
7. U N R Q I E E ______________________
8. Z O N L O E R ______________________
9. B A R G E I L A ______________________
10. S I L U ______________________

Nombre: ______________________________ Fecha: ______________

6 ¿De dónde eres?

You are meeting the following foreign-exchange students who have just arrived at your school. If you ask them where they are from, how would each person respond? Following the model, write their responses in the space provided.

Antonio/Guatemala
Soy de Guatemala.

1. Sonia/México

____

2. Diego/Bolivia

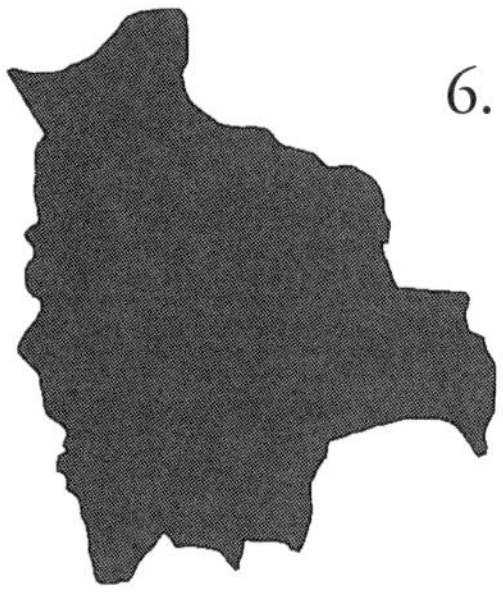

____

3. Mercedes/España

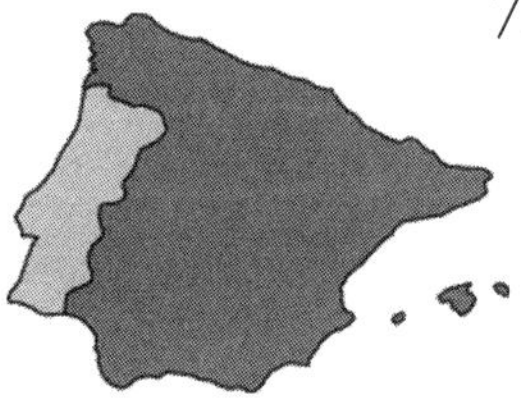

____

4. Luis/la Argentina

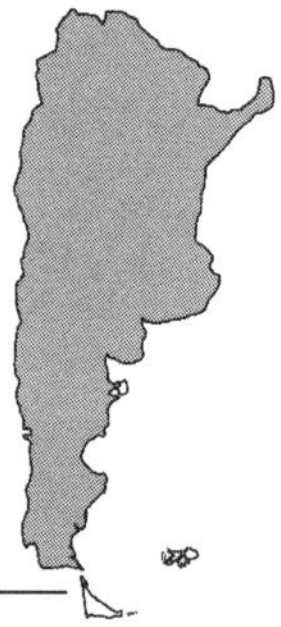

____

5. Armando/Colombia

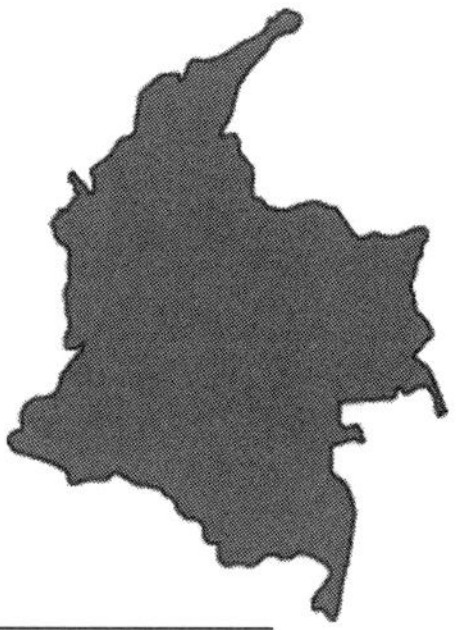

____

6. Ana/Venezuela

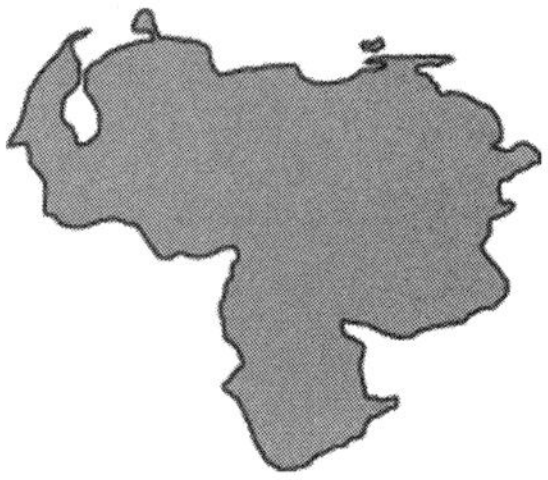

____

7. Sofía/Honduras

____

8. Ernesto/Chile

____

convention where many important people from the Spanish-
red. You introduce yourself to them and ask them where they
y? In the space provided, write the responses in complete

as/España
nio Banderas. Soy de España.

ca Dominica

____

iez /Colombia

____

im /Guatemala

____

4. Chichi Rodríguez /Puerto Rico

____

5. Gloria Estefan /Cuba

____

6. Selma Hayek /México

____

8 ¡Mucho gusto!

Ángela and Mateo meet in the school courtyard. Unscramble their dialog by numbering their statements or questions in a logical order.

______ 1. Me llamo Ángela. ¿Y tú?

______ 2. Mucho gusto, Mateo.

______ 3. No, soy de Bolivia. ¿Y tú?

______ 4. Yo me llamo Mateo.

______ 5. Yo soy de Argentina.

______ 6. ¿Eres tú de aquí?

______ 7. ¡Hola! ¿Cómo te llamas?

9 Más números

Write a number word to answer each math problem.

1 + 1 = dos

1. 1 + 4 = ______________
2. 2 + 6 = ______________
3. 5 - 2 = ______________
4. 3 + 3 = ______________
5. 4 + 7 = ______________
6. 3 x 3 = ______________
7. 8 x 2 = ______________
8. 2 + 2 = ______________

10 Los cognados

While reading your Spanish textbook, you came across words you didn't know but that look familiar to you. Can you guess what they mean? Match the following Spanish words to their English equivalent by writing the appropriate letter in the space provided.

______	1. frase	A. cognate
______	2. parte	B. example
______	3. nación	C. group
______	4. grupo	D. biology
______	5. vocabulario	E. nation
______	6. progreso	F. part
______	7. biología	G. phrase
______	8. ejemplo	H. practice
______	9. práctica	I. progress
______	10. cognado	J. vocabulary

11 Sopa de letras

In the word-square find and circle ten numbers spelled out in Spanish. The words may read forward, backward, vertically, horizontally or diagonally.

D	I	O	S	D	K	L	M	L	K	Q
S	I	E	S	O	R	S	S	D	V	U
O	M	E	E	N	R	D	I	Y	K	I
P	S	I	C	L	E	H	O	E	A	N
N	U	G	S	I	W	N	D	O	T	C
T	X	T	Z	D	S	J	A	W	W	E
C	C	E	R	O	S	É	O	H	C	O
B	Y	Q	A	S	B	G	I	B	N	I
T	A	D	M	L	X	F	I	S	W	E
R	E	T	N	I	E	V	H	M	V	E
E	F	W	J	G	E	P	O	K	G	L
S	A	I	R	H	J	A	O	O	N	U

12 ¿Cuántos años tienes?

You have made new friends in the school cafeteria and have just asked them their age. Following the model, write their responses in the space provided.

Gabriela/18 Tengo dieciocho años.

1. Eva/12______________________
2. Armando/14______________________
3. Elena/16______________________
4. Felipe/13______________________
5. Teresa/17______________________
6. Alejandro/15______________________

13 Diálogo completo

Carolina and Benjamín are meeting for the first time. Fill in the blanks of their conversation below with the appropriate words or phrases. Make sure the dialog follows a logical sequence.

CAROLINA: ¡Hola!

BENJAMÍN: ¡(1)__________! ¿(2)____________________?

CAROLINA: Me llamo Carolina. ¿(3)__________?

BENJAMÍN: Me (4)____________________.

CAROLINA: Mucho gusto Benjamín.

BENJAMÍN: (5)______________. ¿(6)____________________?

CAROLINA: Soy de California ¿(7)__________?

BENJAMÍN: (8)______________ Alaska.

CAROLINA: ¿(9)______________________________?

BENJAMÍN: Tengo (10)______________ años. ¿(11)__________?

CAROLINA: (12)____________________.

BENJAMÍN: Hasta luego.

CAROLINA: (13)______________.

Lección 2

1 No pertenece aquí

Circle the word or expression that does not belong with the other two words or expressions in each row across.

1.	¿Cómo estás?	¿Cómo te llamas?	¿Qué tal?
2.	Regular.	Bien.	cuatro
3.	Gracias.	Mal.	Muy mal.
4.	¿Qué tal?	¿Cuántos años tienes?	¿Cómo estás?
5.	Hasta luego.	Adiós.	Muy bien.

2 Saludos

Are the following expressions appropriate to greet a friend or an acquaintance? Indicate which of the following expressions are formal and which are informal. Write the letter **F** for *formal* or **I** for *informal* in the space provided.

1. ______ ¿Cómo está Ud.?
2. ______ Buenos días.
3. ______ ¡Hola!
4. ______ ¿Qué tal?
5. ______ Buenas tardes.
6. ______ ¿Cómo estás?
7. ______ ¿Cómo están?

Nombre: ______________________________ Fecha: ________________

3 Tú, Ud., Uds., vosotros y vosotras

The students, faculty and staff at your school have gathered to celebrate the beginning of the new school year. How would you address the following people? Fill in the blank with the appropriate subject pronoun. Write *tú*, *Ud.*, *Uds.*, *vosotros* or *vosotras* in the space provided.

a friend: tú

1. a classmate: ________________
2. the principal at school: ________________
3. the bus driver: ________________
4. the parents of a classmate: ________________
5. Pilar and Blanca, your friends from Spain: ________________
6. your sister: ________________
7. José and Tomás, your friends from México: ________________

4 Los apodos

You are given a list of the names of your classmates. Since you know them only by their nicknames, or *apodos,* you need to figure out who is who. Match the nickname on the right with the name on the left by writing the appropriate letter in the space provided.

1. ______	Guadalupe	A. Fina
2. ______	Francisco	B. Pepe
3. ______	José	C. Quique
4. ______	Josefina	D. Lupe
5. ______	Isabel	E. Isa
6. ______	Enrique	F. Paco

5 Saludos y despedidas

The two friends in the pictures below have just run into each other on the street. Think of what they might be saying to each other. Write the expressions that best fit the situation inside the speech bubbles. Be creative!

Nombre: ______________________________ Fecha: ______________

6 Crucigrama

Complete the following crossword puzzle with the correct spelling of the numbers provided.

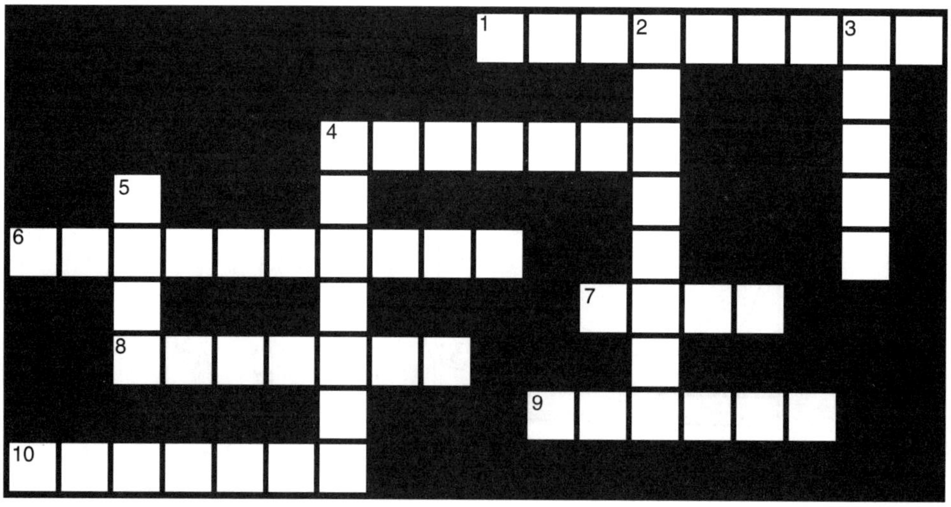

Horizontales

1. 50
4. 70
6. 26
7. 11
8. 90
9. 4
10. 30

Verticales

2. 40
3. 13
4. 60
5. 100

7 ¿Cuántos euros?

The new currency in Europe is the euro. Imagine that you have gone to the bank to exchange money and you count it to make sure you have the correct amount. How many euros do you have in each instance? Write your answer in Spanish.

1. ______________________

2. ______________________

3. ______________________

4. ______________________

5. ______________________

6. ______________________

8 Los números de teléfono

Imagine that you are at a meeting with several classmates and you are in charge of making a list of telephone numbers. Your classmates give their names and telephone numbers in turn. What do they say? Write what each person might say, following the model.

Rodríguez, Verónica/12-23-34
Verónica Rodríguez, doce, veintitrés, treinta y cuatro

1. Montalbán, Cecilia/38-93-56

____

____

2. Pineda, José/79-47-82

____

____

3. González, Nicanor/63-73-40

____

____

4. Perales, Alicia/78-24-98

____

____

5. Herrera, María/56-36-97

____

____

9 ¿Qué hora es?

Each clock indicates a different time. What time is it? Look at the clocks shown and write the correct time in the space provided.

Son las once menos diez.

1. ______________________________

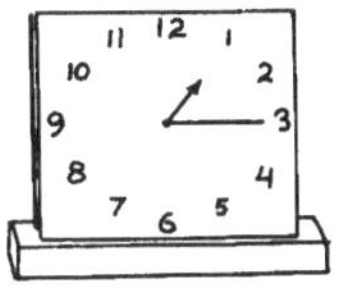

2. ______________________________

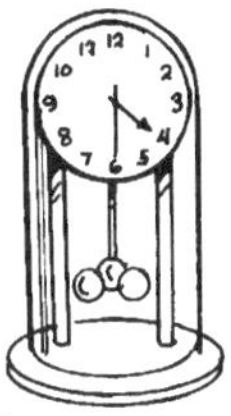

3. ______________________________

4. ______________________________

5. ______________________________

6. ______________________________

7. ______________________________

8. ______________________________

10 La mañana, la tarde y la noche

In many countries in Europe and Latin America a 24-hour clock is used instead of the 12-hour clock with the A.M. and P.M. designators. In this system, 14:00 is the same 2:00 P.M. or two o'clock in the afternoon. Following the model sentence, write out the times indicated on the clocks. Use the time expressions, *de la mañana, de la tarde, de la noche.*

Son las dos de la tarde.

1. ____

2. ____

3. ____

4. ____

5. ____

6. ____

7. ____

8. ____

Nombre: ______________________ Fecha: ______________

11 La geografía y la hora

Did you know that there are different time zones throughout the world? Look at the following map showing various time zones. Can you tell which Spanish-speaking countries share the same time zone? Use the clocks at the bottom of the map to help you answer the questions.

Es mediodía en España. ¿Y en Cuba?
Son las siete de la mañana en Cuba.

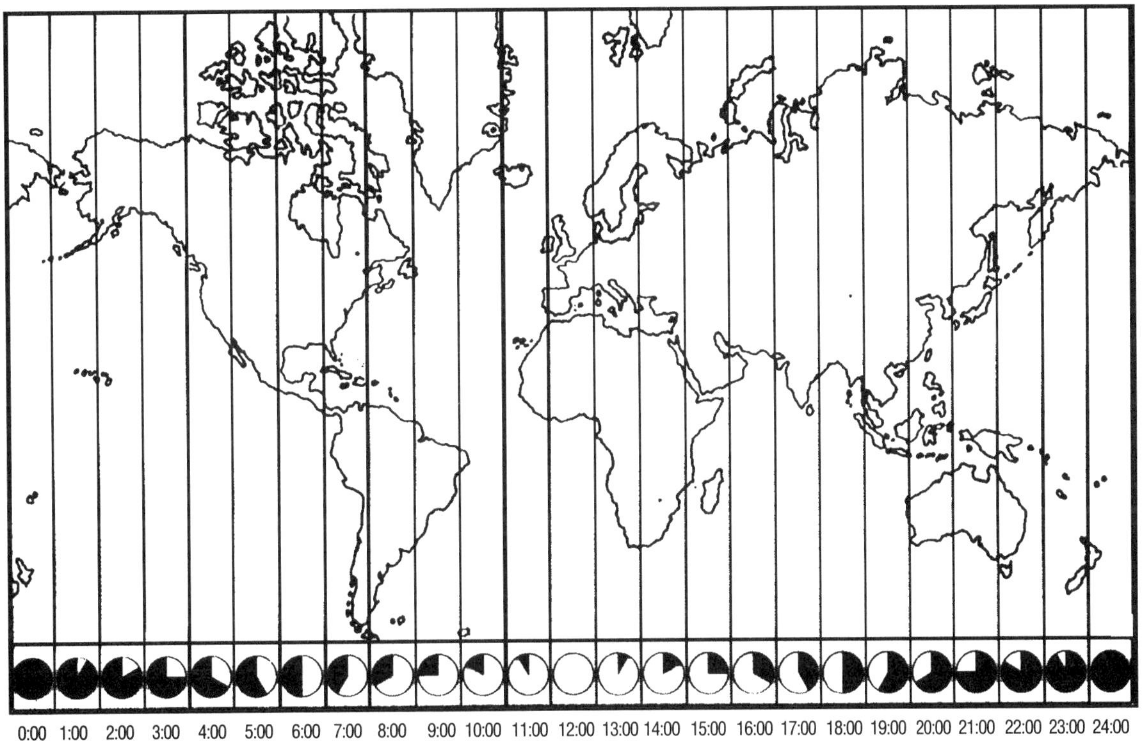

1. Es la una de la tarde en Guinea Ecuatorial. ¿Y en España?

____

2. Son las cinco de la mañana en México, D.F. ¿Y en Bolivia?

____

3. Son las ocho de la mañana en Argentina. ¿Y en Venezuela?

____

4. Son las seis de la mañana en Guatemala. ¿Y en Uruguay?

____

5. Son las siete de la mañana en la República Dominicana. ¿Y en Costa Rica?

____

12 Por favor

It is a busy day at the supermarket. Look at the people in the drawings and imagine what you would say in each situation. Write an appropriate expression in the empty speech bubbles.

Por favor.	Con mucho gusto.	Lo siento.

1.

2.

3.

13 Dialogo completo

Sandra and Tomás are sitting across the table from you in the school cafeteria and you overhear part of their conversation. Can you figure out the expressions you did not hear? Write them in the blank spaces of the dialog below.

SANDRA: ¡(1)____________________!

TOMÁS: ¡Hola! ¿(2)________________?

SANDRA: Bien. ¿(3)________________?

TOMÁS: Regular.

SANDRA: ¿(4)____________________?

TOMÁS: (5)____________________dos y veinte de la tarde.

SANDRA: Hasta luego.

TOMÁS: (6)____________________.

Nombre: ______________________ Fecha: ______________

CAPÍTULO 2

Lección 3

1 ¿Qué quiere decir?

Have you noticed how many places in the southwestern United States have Spanish names? Look at the following list of place names that come from the Spanish language and try to guess what they mean. Use a Spanish-English dictionary or an encyclopedia to match the words on the left with the words on the right. Write the letter of your answer choice in the space provided.

1. ______	California	A.	a fictional island of great wealth
2. ______	Colorado	B.	big river
3. ______	Nevada	C.	humid lowlands
4. ______	Montana	D.	mountain
5. ______	Río Grande	E.	poplars (a type of tree)
6. ______	Amarillo, TX	F.	red
7. ______	Los Álamos, NM	G.	St. Anthony
8. ______	San Antonio, TX	H.	snowy
9. ______	San Francisco, CA	I.	St. Francis
10. ______	San José, CA	J.	St. Joseph
11. ______	Pueblo, CO	K.	table or hill with level top
12. ______	Mesa, AZ	L.	the pass
13. ______	Las Vegas, NV	M.	town or people
14. ______	El Paso, TX	N.	yellow

Nombre: ______________________________ Fecha: ______________

2 Geografía

You need to prepare a report for your geography class about places with Spanish names in the United States. Begin your research by locating the following states and rivers on the map provided.

California
Colorado
Colorado River
Montana
Nevada
Río Grande

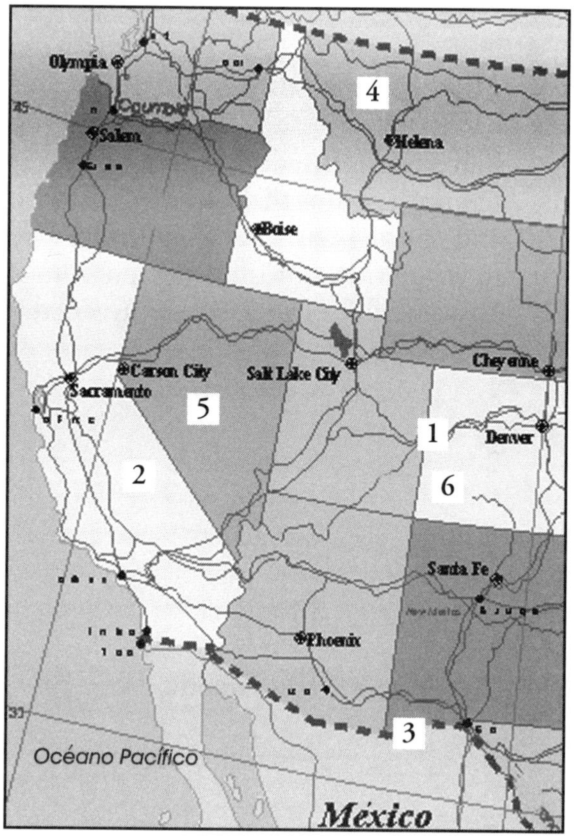

1. ______________
2. ______________
3. ______________
4. ______________
5. ______________
6. ______________

3 Tú, él, ella y yo

Your new classmate, Alejandro, is meeting Beatriz, another student, for the first time. He asks her questions about herself and some other students standing nearby. Help Alejandro and Beatriz use the appropriate subject pronouns by writing them in the spaces provided in the dialog. Some pronouns may be used more than once.

tú él ella yo

ALEJANDRO: ¡Hola! ¿Cómo te llamas (1)______?

BEATRIZ: (2)______ me llamo Beatriz.

ALEJANDRO: ¿Cómo se llama (3)______?

BEATRIZ: Se llama Ricardo.

ALEJANDRO: ¿De dónde es (4)______?

BEATRIZ: Es de Venezuela.

ALEJANDRO: ¿Y (5)______?

BEATRIZ: Laura es de Panamá.

BEATRIZ: Y (6)______, ¿cómo te llamas?

ALEJANDRO: (7)______ me llamo Alejandro.

4 Hablando por teléfono

Fernando is talking on the telephone. Apparently, the person with whom he is speaking wants to know about classes, teachers, and the other students at Fernando's school. Complete what Fernando is saying during the conversation with the appropriate forms of the verb *ser.*

1. Hola, Carla. Yo __________ Fernando.
2. Sí, Graciela y yo __________ estudiantes de la profesora Cifuentes.
3. Mi amigo se llama Jorge. Él __________ de Nicaragua.
4. Los amigos de Jorge __________ de Chile.
5. Yo __________ de Los Ángeles.
6. Mi padre __________ de Venezuela.
7. Los profesores de español no __________ de aquí.
8. Ellos __________ de México.
9. Y tú, ¿de dónde __________ ?
10. ¿ __________ tú una estudiante nueva?

Nombre: ______________________ Fecha: ______________

5 ¿Cómo se llama y de dónde es?

Look at the map that follows and tell where each person is from?

Nicolás es de Managua, Nicaragua.

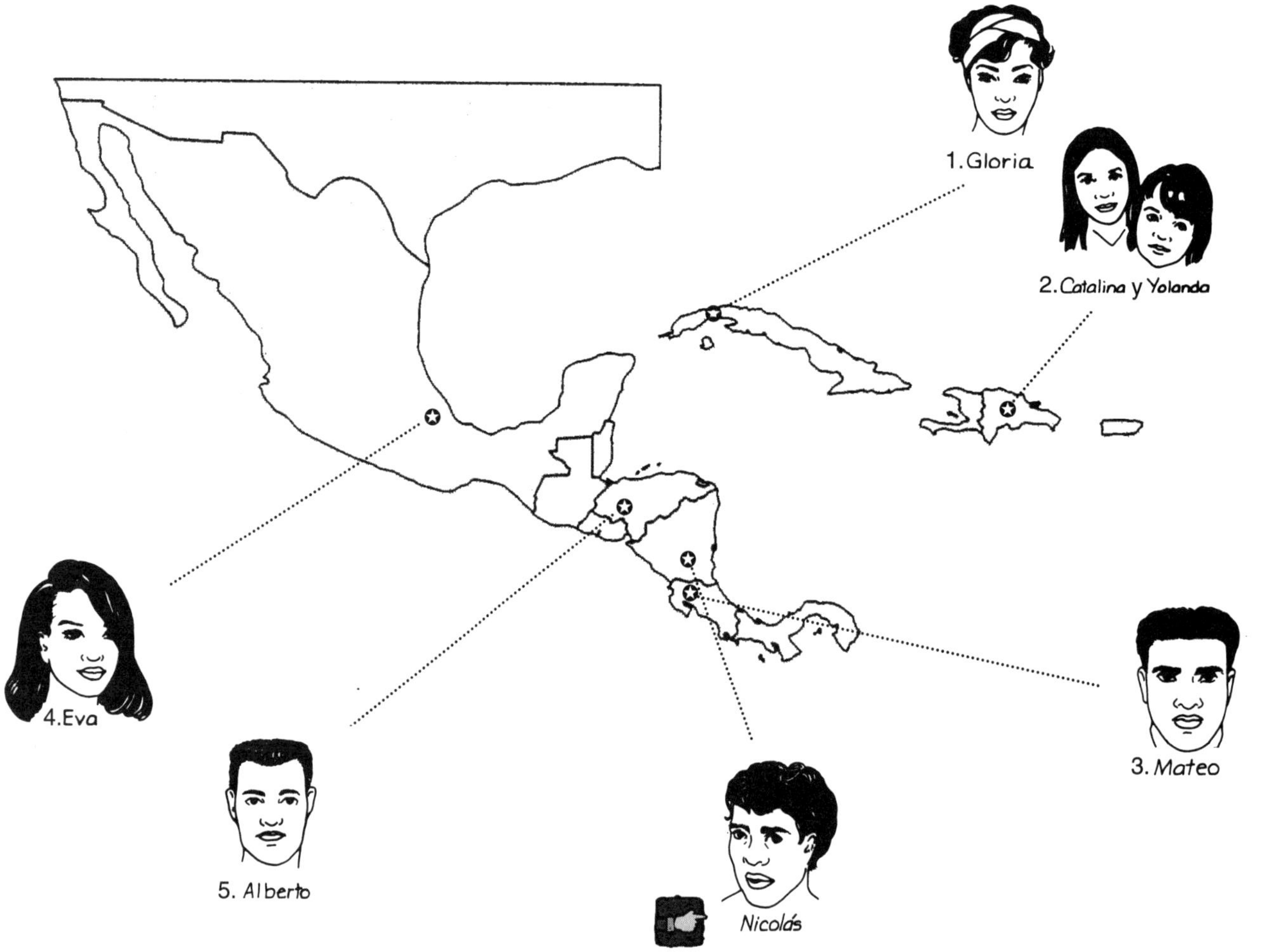

1. ______________________
2. ______________________
3. ______________________
4. ______________________
5. ______________________

Nombre: ______________________________ Fecha: ______________

6 Personas famosas

While playing a trivia game with some of your classmates, you have drew cards with the names of several famous people. Use the Internet or the library to find out where they are from.

Celia Cruz
Es de Cuba.

República Dominicana
México
España
Cuba
Panamá
Chile
COLOMBIA

1. Pablo Picasso

____

2. Gabriel García Márquez

____

3. Antonio Banderas

____

4. Frida Kahlo

____

5. Isabel Allende

____

7 ¿Qué es?

Look at the following illustrations and write complete sentences to identify each object. Be sure to include the appropriate definite article in the space provided.

Es el cesto de papeles. 

1. ______________________________

3. ______________________________

2. ______________________________

4. ______________________________

8 En la clase

It is your first day at a new school and you meet the new students in your class. Since you do not know their names, identify them by the objects they are holding. Follow the model.

Rosario
La estudiante con el lápiz se llama Rosario.

1. Federico

____

____

2. Carla

____

____

3. Tomás

____

____

4. Gabriela

____

____

5. Andrés

____

____

6. Josefina

____

____

7. Esteban

____

____

8. Virginia

____

____

9 Masculino o femenino

Find and circle the word in each row that does not match the gender of the others.

1.	amiga	puerta	señor
2.	silla	chico	pupitre
3.	revista	libro	mapa
4.	mochila	cesto de papeles	profesor
5.	sacapuntas	lápiz	página
6.	puerta	bolígrafo	ventana

10 Las computadoras

Skim the article to find out what it says and then find 10 nouns and circle them.

¿Estudias, trabajas o interneteas?

Acer presenta la nueva generación de portátiles, más joven, emprendedora y con mayores prestaciones. Sin duda, el portátil que buscas.

Está claro, no todo el mundo utiliza su portátil para lo mismo. Hay quien lo necesita para estudiar, para navegar por Internet, para desmadrarse con el último juego multimedia del mercado o, evidentemente, como una herramienta de trabajo.

Por eso, Acer, uno de los más grandes fabricantes del mundo, y la 2ª marca más vendida en España, tiene portátiles para todos. Por ejemplo, el Acer Extensa™ 355, el más asequible del mercado, pero todo un monstruo en prestaciones, que además acepta ampliaciones como un CD-Rom externo. Después está el Acer Extensa™ 390. Un cerebro que sólo pesa 2,9 Kg. para llevarlo a todas partes, para conectarlo en la oficina o trabajar en tu casa. Con todas las aplicaciones multimedia y una increíble pantalla de alta resolución. Y si eres de los que viajan, con el Acer TravelMate™ 7100 puedes montarte la oficina en cualquier parte, porque tiene un procesador Intel Pentium® con Tecnología MMX™ a 266 MHz. y una batería con una duración de hasta 10 horas. Una joya. Si quieres saber más, conecta con Acer: http://www.acer.es o llámanos al 902 20 23 23.

11 No, no, no

Imagine you have received an e-mail by mistake. After reading the message you realize it is not for you. Using negative responses, write out the answers to each question for the e-mail you received. The first statement has been done for you.

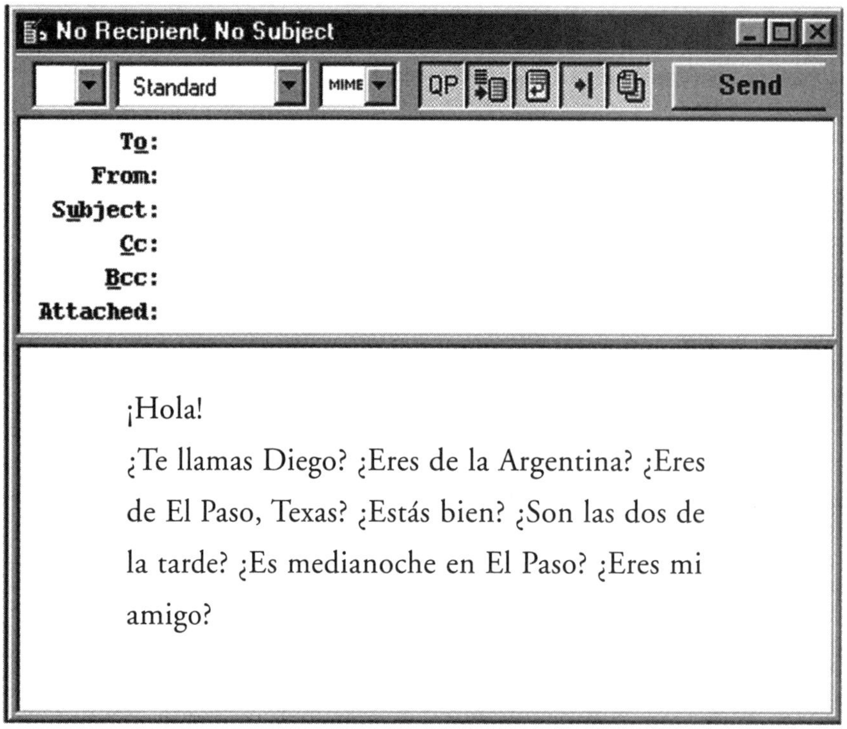

No me llamo Diego.

____

____

____

____

____

____

Nombre: ______________________ Fecha: ______________

12 Plurales

Look at the illustration and write complete sentences to identify the numbered objects. Make sure to include the appropriate definite article for each object.

Son los cuadernos.

1. ______________________
2. ______________________
3. ______________________
4. ______________________
5. ______________________
6. ______________________
7. ______________________

Nombre: ______________________ Fecha: ______________

13 Lista de objetos

Make an inventory of the objects in your classroom and write a list in the space provided. Be sure to include the appropriate indefinite articles. The first one has been done for you.

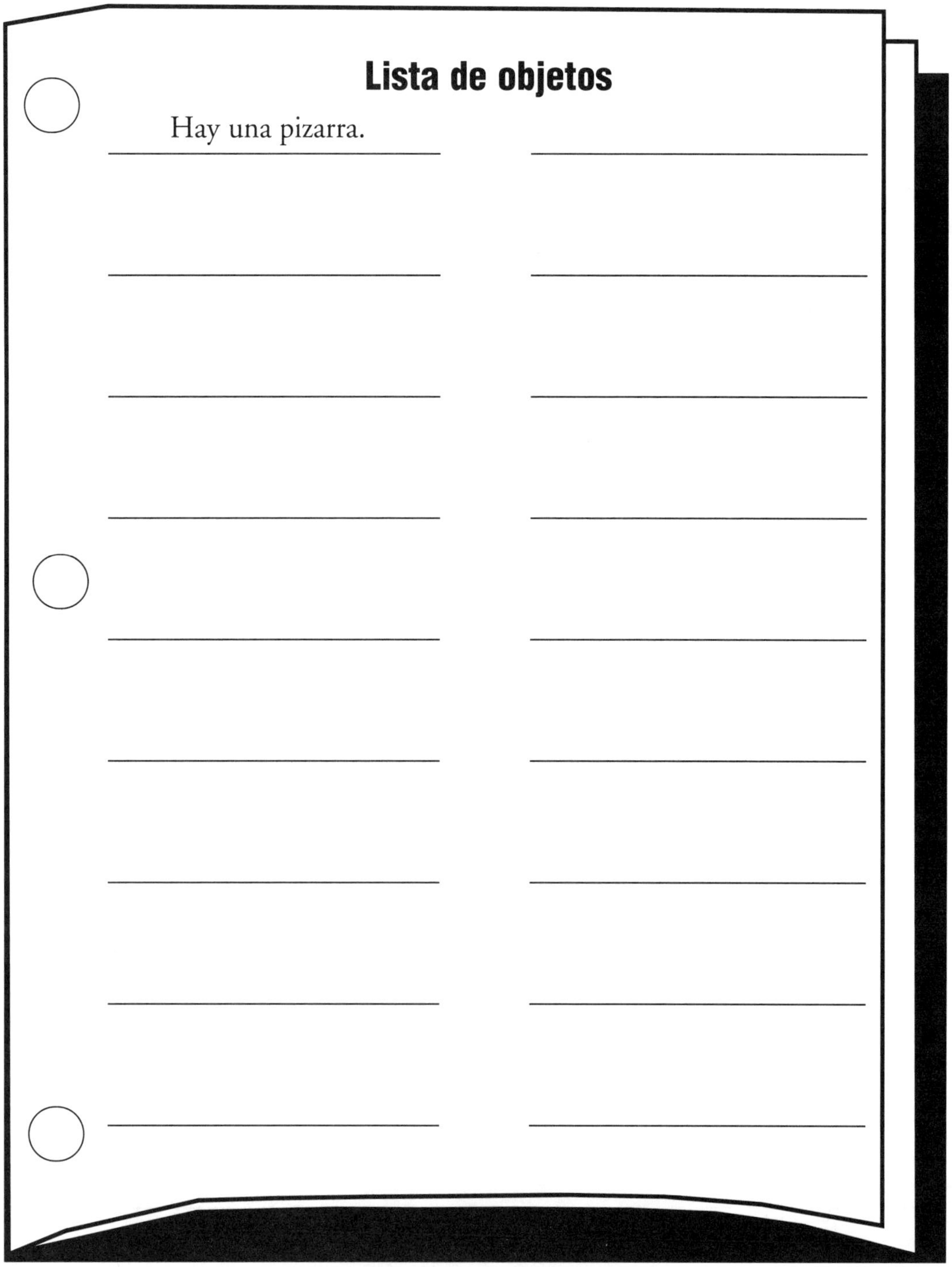

Nombre: ______________________ Fecha: ______________

Lección 4

1 El horario de clases

Complete Juan's class schedule with the correct class for each time and day of the week. Use the information given below.

	LUNES	MARTES	MIÉRCOLES	JUEVES	VIERNES
8:15					
9:05					
9:55					
10:45					
11:35					
12:25					
1:15					
2:05					

1. La clase de computación de Juan es de lunes a viernes a las once y treinta y cinco de la mañana.
2. Hay almuerzo de lunes a viernes a las doce y veinticinco de la tarde.
3. Hay clase de español de lunes a viernes a la una y cuarto de la tarde.
4. Hay clase de biología de lunes a viernes a las nueve y cincuenta y cinco de la mañana.
5. Tambien hay clase de biología los miércoles a las diez y cuarenta y cinco de la mañana.
6. La clase de historia de Juan es a las ocho y quince de la mañana de lunes a viernes.
7. Hay clase de música a las dos y cinco de la tarde los lunes, martes y miércoles.
8. Hay clase de inglés los lunes, martes, jueves y viernes a las once menos cuarto de la mañana.
9. La clase de arte de Juan es a las dos y cinco de la tarde los jueves y viernes.
10. Hay clase de matemáticas a las nueve y cinco de la mañana de lunes a viernes.

Nombre: ______________________________ Fecha: ______________

2 Sopa de letras

Circle in the word-square puzzle seven names of colors. The words may appear forward, backward, horizontally, vertically or diagonally.

O	C	L	F	É	Z	E	D	A	Z	W
J	W	S	V	U	D	O	S	R	O	E
O	T	N	O	R	E	T	B	O	S	I
R	O	P	E	L	N	V	L	D	B	O
A	R	V	U	G	R	I	S	A	L	L
R	A	R	T	I	R	N	J	E	A	L
O	P	D	G	A	H	O	D	O	N	I
S	E	O	M	J	I	T	C	R	C	R
A	N	K	R	A	N	J	A	E	O	A
D	X	Z	K	Y	Q	I	N	E	G	M
O	L	S	A	Z	U	L	U	S	T	A

Nombre: ______________________________ Fecha: ________________

3 ¿De quién es?

Imagine that you are responsible for the lost-and-found box at your school, and the following items have been found. Follow the model to determine who owns each item.

la mochila	el libro	el cuaderno	el mapa	el bolígrafo
la revista	el reloj	el sacapuntas	la regla	

Es la mochila de Mónica.

Mónica

1. Cristina ______________________________

2. Carlos ______________________________

3. Josefina ______________________________

4. Gloria ______________________________

5. Lorenzo ______________________________

6. Benjamín ______________________________

Nombre: ______________________________ Fecha: ______________

4 Hay una silla verde

Make a list of the objects shown in the box. Then find them in your classroom and state what color they are.

1. ______________________________.

2. ______________________________.

3. ______________________________.

4. ______________________________.

5. ______________________________.

6. ______________________________.

7. ______________________________.

8. ______________________________.

5 ¿Qué hacen ellos?

Write the appropriate form of the verb that best completes each sentence.

estudiar hablar terminar necesitar

1. Carmen____________________ matemáticas.
2. Yo____________________ un lápiz nuevo.
3. La señorita Martínez____________________ español muy bien.
4. Los estudiantes____________________ los libros de historia.
5. La clase de Graciela____________________ a las ocho.
6. Juan y yo____________________ con el profesor Fernández.
7. ¿Cuándo____________________ el libro de Carlos Fuentes?
8. Pepe y Jaime____________________ computación.

6 ¿Cuándo estudias?

Complete the following dialog with the appropriate form of *estudiar* when referring to studying or with *a las* when referring to the time.

RAÚL: Hola.

TÚ: Hola. ¿Cómo estás?

RAÚL: Estoy bien. Tengo muchas clases.

TÚ: ¿Cuándo (1)____________________ tú?

RAÚL: Yo estudio a las nueve de la noche. ¿Y tú?

TÚ: Yo (2)____________________ a las siete y media y mi hermana (3)____________________ ocho. Ella y sus amigas (4)____________________ biología.

RAÚL: ¿A qué hora (5)____________________ tú español?

TÚ: Yo estudio (6)____________________ ocho de la noche.

RAÚL: ¿A qué hora terminas de (7)____________________?

TÚ: A las nueve de la noche.

7 Las calificaciones

A friend of yours would like to apply to a school in Mexico and has asked you to translate her school records to Spanish. You have the grades as percentages and you wish to convert them to the grading scale used in many Spanish-speaking countries (shown in this chart). Write the letter of your choice in the space provided. Note: Some grade assignations may be repeated.

______ 1. 100% en historia

______ 2. 40% en inglés

______ 3. 60% en computación

______ 4. 70% en español

______ 5. 100% en música

______ 6. 80% en matemáticas

______ 7. 90% en biología

______ 8. 50% en arte

CALIFICACIONES		
S	Superior	10
EX	Excelente	9
MB	Muy Bueno	8
B	Bueno	7-6
NM	Necesita mejorar	5
D	Deficiente	4-0

8 ¿Dónde está?

Practice your geography skills in Spanish and write questions and answers using the correct form of *estar*. You may use an atlas or the Internet for help.

Amarillo y San Ángelo
Amarillo y San Ángelo están en Texas.

1. Los Álamos y Las Cruces

____

2. Mesa

____

3. San Antonio, El Paso y Del Río

____

4. Santa Fe

____

5. San Francisco, Los Ángeles y Sacramento

____

6. Las Vegas

____

7. Pueblo

____

9 En la clase de computación

Send an e-mail to a friend in Spain. Complete the message (*mensaje*) using the appropriate words from the list below.

necesitas estás ESTOY terminas
termina están necesito estamos

No Recipient, No Subject

Standard MIME QP Send

To:
From:
Subject:
Cc:
Bcc:
Attached:

¡Hola!

Yo (1)________________ en la clase de computación. Mis amigos

(2)________________en la clase de español. ¿Cómo (3)________________

tú? Nosotros (4)________________ muy bien. La clase

(5)________________ en treinta minutos

y yo (6)________________ terminar el mensaje. ¿A qué hora

(7)________________con tus clases? ¿(8)________________ estudiar mucho?

10 En mi clase de español

Look at the illustration of a computer class below and answer the questions that follow.

¿Cuantos libros hay?
Hay un libro.

1. ¿Cuántos estudiantes hay?

2. ¿Cuántas computadoras hay?

3. ¿Cuántos profesores hay?

4. ¿Dónde está el reloj?

5. ¿Hay un ratón?

6. ¿Cuántos diskettes hay en el escritorio?

11 En la Internet

While surfing the Internet you have found the Web page of a technical institute that carries out safety research on cars. Skim this page and circle the words in the text that refer to color. Then answer the questions.

Coches: los colores más seguros

Europa en rojo

COLORES PREFERIDOS EN EUROPA (%)	ROJO	NEGRO	AZUL	BLANCO	VERDE	PLATA
BÉLGICA	12	10	11	6	7	7
FRANCIA	11	13	6	11	7	6
ALEMANIA	16	13	11	5	3	5
HOLANDA	18	10	9	2	6	2
ITALIA	17	13	11	12	6	8
PORTUGAL	32	17	7	10	5	12
ESPAÑA	21	9	8	21	4	6
SUIZA	11	6	8	6	2	3
INGLATERRA	18	11	17	8	10	4
GRECIA	23	22	10	18	4	4
PROMEDIO	17	12	10	9	6	6

Fuente: Car & Driver, febrero

Para los europeos, el color representa un 1% en su escala de valores a la hora de elegir un vehículo, y su diseño es tenido en cuenta en un 4%. El rojo es el preferido por el 17% de los usuarios, mientras que el verde y el plateado son los menos seleccionados.

1. What is the favorite color in Belgium ?

   ____

2. What color do people in France prefer?

   ____

3. What are the two favorite colors in Spain?

   ____

4. What color do people in England prefer?

   ____

12 El reportaje

A reporter for a teen magazine is interviewing students. Answer his personal questions using complete sentences.

1. ¿Cómo te llamas?

2. ¿Cuál es tu número de teléfono?

3. ¿Cómo se llama tu colegio?

4. ¿Cuántas clases hay en tu horario?

5. ¿Qué clases tienes los lunes?

6. ¿Qué días tienes clases de español?

7. ¿De qué color son las paredes de tu clase?

Nombre: ______________________ Fecha: ______________

CAPÍTULO 3

Lección 5

1 Crucigrama

Complete the following crossword puzzle with the expressions you have learned for introducing people in Spanish.

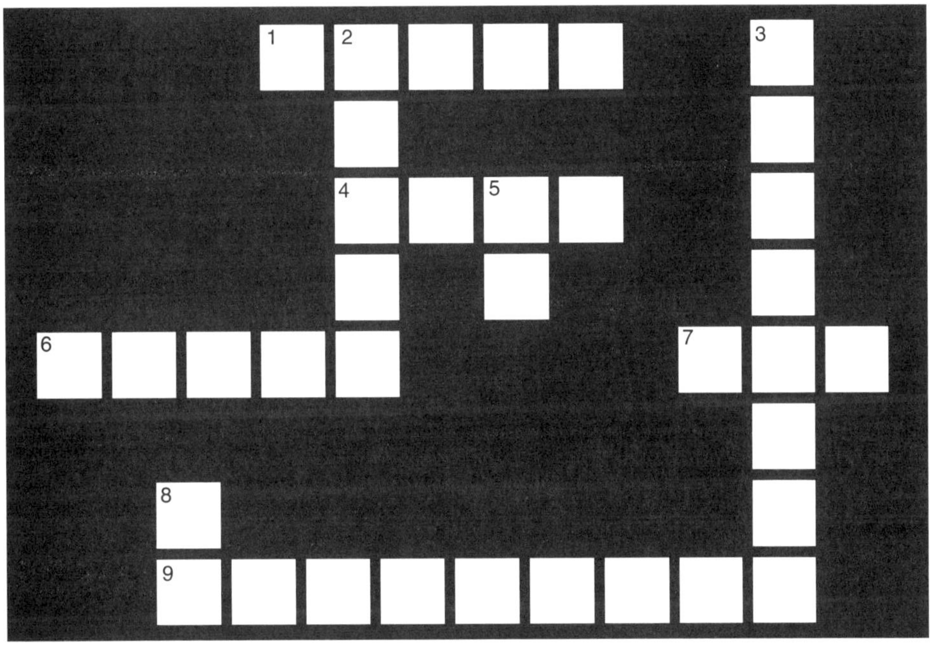

Horizontales

1. Te presento a mi _ , Juan.
4. ¿_ estás?
6. Mucho _.
7. _ presento al Sr. Cerezo.
9. _ ,Sr. Cerezo.

Verticales

2. _ gusto.
3. Les _ a mi profesor de español.
5. Te presento a _ amiga, Paula.
8. _ presento a mi amigo, Manuel.

2 En la fiesta

You are hosting a Spanish club party at your house. In order to find out how to introduce people to one another, unscramble and write out these sentences.

a/mi amiga/te/presento
Te presento a mi amiga.

1. Carlos/a/Sra. Fernández/le presento

____

2. español/de/profesora/la señorita/Santini/mi/le presento/a

____

3. Sandra/les presento/a/mi/amiga

____

4. presento/a/la amiga/te/Antonio/de

____

5. a/les/Josefina/presento/Sr. y Sra Carranza

____

6. te/mi/presento/a/amigo

____

7. a/el Sr. Vallejo/les/presento/mi profesor

____

8. a/le presento/matemáticas/mi profesor/de

____

3 Otras presentaciones

Several new people have arrived to the party and you wish to introduce them. Fill in the blanks with *a, a la, al, de, de la* or *del.*

Rogelio, te presento a la amiga de Margarita.

1. Carmen, te presento __________ profesor de Juan Carlos.
2. Le presento a doña Lola, la amiga __________ señor Buñuel.
3. Les presento a la amiga __________ doña Lola.
4. Le presento __________ amiga de mi profesora.
5. Les presento __________ señor Valverde, mi profesor de computación.
6. Te presento __________ amiga de Carlota.
7. Sr. y Sra. Vargas, les presento __________ profesora de música.
8. Te presento __________ Margarita, la amiga __________ estudiante nuevo.

4 Presentaciones

Look at the following drawing. Catalina is introducing a new student named Isabel to the teacher, Srta. Corinto. Complete the dialog with the appropriate expressions.

5 Buscando información en la Internet

You are planning a trip to Mexico City and you have found a Web page that gives you information about cultural events in that city. Skim the information provided on the site and write answers to the following questions.

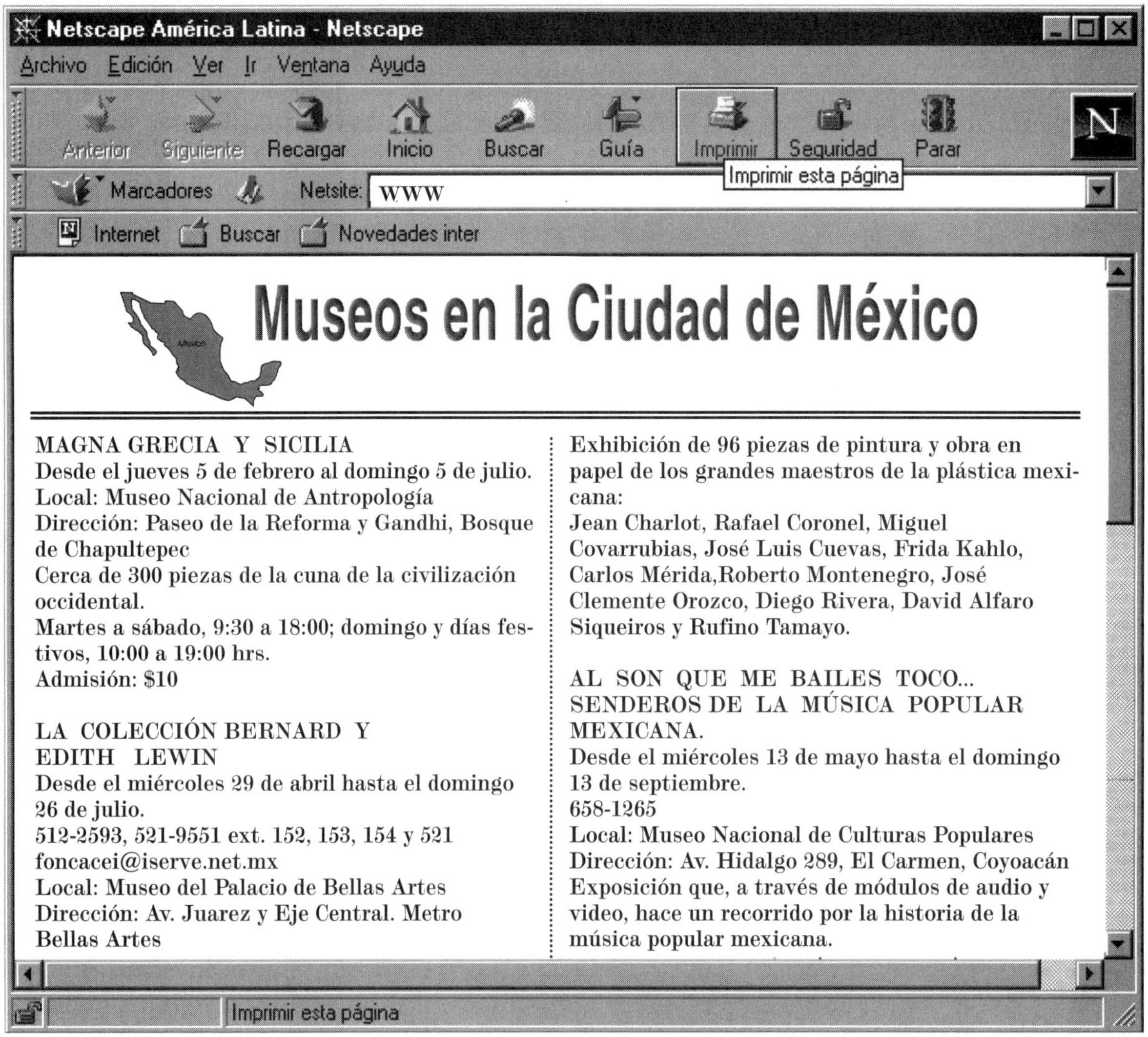

Museos en la Ciudad de México

MAGNA GRECIA Y SICILIA
Desde el jueves 5 de febrero al domingo 5 de julio.
Local: Museo Nacional de Antropología
Dirección: Paseo de la Reforma y Gandhi, Bosque de Chapultepec
Cerca de 300 piezas de la cuna de la civilización occidental.
Martes a sábado, 9:30 a 18:00; domingo y días festivos, 10:00 a 19:00 hrs.
Admisión: $10

LA COLECCIÓN BERNARD Y EDITH LEWIN
Desde el miércoles 29 de abril hasta el domingo 26 de julio.
512-2593, 521-9551 ext. 152, 153, 154 y 521
foncacei@iserve.net.mx
Local: Museo del Palacio de Bellas Artes
Dirección: Av. Juarez y Eje Central. Metro Bellas Artes
Exhibición de 96 piezas de pintura y obra en papel de los grandes maestros de la plástica mexicana:
Jean Charlot, Rafael Coronel, Miguel Covarrubias, José Luis Cuevas, Frida Kahlo, Carlos Mérida, Roberto Montenegro, José Clemente Orozco, Diego Rivera, David Alfaro Siqueiros y Rufino Tamayo.

AL SON QUE ME BAILES TOCO... SENDEROS DE LA MÚSICA POPULAR MEXICANA.
Desde el miércoles 13 de mayo hasta el domingo 13 de septiembre.
658-1265
Local: Museo Nacional de Culturas Populares
Dirección: Av. Hidalgo 289, El Carmen, Coyoacán
Exposición que, a través de módulos de audio y video, hace un recorrido por la historia de la música popular mexicana.

1. Where would you go if you wanted to see art by Frida Kahlo?

____

2. What is the name of that exhibit?

____

3. What dates is it open?

____

4. What exhibit is held at the Museo Nacional de Antropología?

____

5. Where is the Museo Nacional de Antropología?

____

6. Where would you go to find out about popular Mexican music?

____

7. What is the telephone number of the Museo Nacional de Culturas Populares?

____

8. What is the name of the exhibit at the Museo Nacional de Culturas Populares?

____

6 ¿Van a la fiesta?

There is a party at school next week and you overhear two students talking about it. What are they saying? Match the questions to the corresponding answers.

______ 1. ¿Va el chico nuevo a la fiesta?

______ 2. ¿Va doña Justina a la fiesta?

______ 3. ¿Va Jorge a la fiesta?

______ 4. ¿Es grande la fiesta?

______ 5. ¿Va Josefina a la fiesta?

______ 6. ¿Vamos a la fiesta?

______ 7. ¿Van tus amigos a la fiesta?

______ 8. ¿Es a las ocho la fiesta?

A. No, la fiesta no es a las ocho. Es a las siete.

B. Sí, la fiesta es grande.

C. Sí, Jorge va a la fiesta.

D. Sí, doña Justina va a la fiesta.

E. Sí, el chico nuevo va a la fiesta.

F. No, Josefina no va.

G. Sí, claro. ¡Vamos!

H. Sí, mis amigos van a la fiesta.

Nombre: ______________________________ Fecha: ______________

7 La fiesta del club

You are an assistant at the local public radio station and you have been assigned to interview the Spanish club president about a party the club has organized at the high school. Look at the advertisement and write questions about the party for your interview. Use the answers provided to help you to write the appropriate question for each answer.

El sábado 13 de marzo

¡Gran Fiesta Estudiantil!

En el gimnasio del Colegio Los Delfines.

¡A Bailar con la música del grupo musical

¡Los Van y Vienen!

Costo: $20 por pareja

De las 18:00 a las 22:00 horas.

Para más información llamar al Tel. 555-1234

Sólo se admiten estudiantes del Colegio Los Delfines y sus invitados.

1. ____

   ____

   Es el sábado, 13 de marzo.

2. ____

   ____

   Es en el gimnasio del Colegio Los Delfines.

3. ____

   ____

   Es a las 18:00.

4. ____

   ____

   El grupo de música se llama **¡Los Van y Vienen!**

5. ____

   ____

   El número de teléfono es el 555-1234.

6. ____

   ____

   Sólo van estudiantes del Colegio Los Delfines y sus invitados.

8 ¿Por qué no van a la fiesta?

Hernán has received a note from Esteban and Carolina saying that they cannot go to the party. Read their note to find out why they cannot attend. Rain has smudged the writing on the paper, and words are missing. To help Hernán understand the note, fill in the blanks with the correct forms of the verb *ir.*

¡Hola!

Nosotros no (1)__________ a la fiesta. Carolina no (2)__________ porque (3)__________ al cine con María. Yo no (4)__________ tampoco porque (5)__________ a México con el profesor Gómez. Nosotros (6)__________ a Monterrey. Jorge y Sara, los estudiantes nuevos, sí (7)__________ porque ellos tienen transporte. ¿Y tú? ¿(8)__________ a la fiesta?

Hasta luego.

Carolina y Esteban

Nombre: ______________________________ Fecha: ______________

9 ¿Adónde van?

You meet a number of people going to different places. Write complete sentences using the correct form of the verb *ir*, to tell where each person is going.

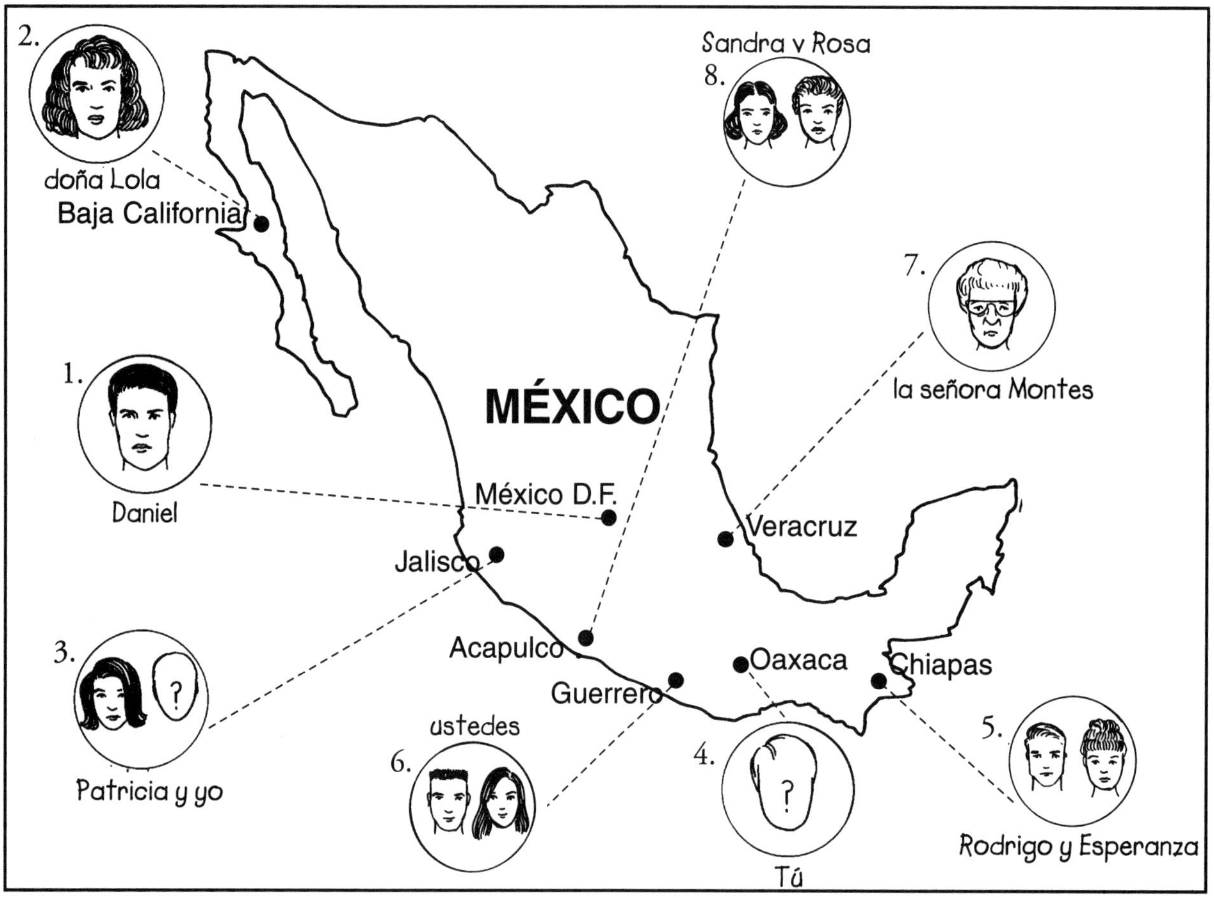

1. Daniel

____

2. doña Lola

____

3. Patricia y yo

____

4. tú

____

5. Rodrigo y Esperanza

____

6. ustedes

____

7. la señora Montes

____

8. Sandra y Rosa

____

10 ¿Adónde va?

Where are the following people going? Read the following phrases in English on the left and then match them with the appropriate phrases in Spanish on the right. Write the correct letter in the space provided.

______	1. Diego needs to check out a book.	A. Va a la biblioteca.
______	2. Don Gustavo needs to cash a check.	B. Va a la cafetería.
______	3. Elisa wants to watch a movie.	C. Va a la escuela.
______	4. Eva feels ill.	D. Va a la oficina.
______	5. Luis has a bad tooth.	E. Va al banco.
______	6. Paula is hungry.	F. Va al cine.
______	7. Profesora Serrano teaches Spanish.	G. Va al dentista.
______	8. Raquel wants to have a picnic.	H. Va al médico.
______	9. Señor Ramírez has to go to work.	I. Va al parque.

11 ¿Adónde van a ir mañana?

Where are you and your friends going tomorrow? Combine words from the three columns to form complete sentences in Spanish. Add any necessary words and make changes as needed.

Mis amigos van a ir al dentista a las tres de la tarde.

Amalia	biblioteca	3:00 P.M.
El chico nuevo	cine	5:30 P.M.
Isabel y yo	médico	11:00 A.M.
mi amiga	banco	10:15 P.M.
Raúl y Esperanza	restaurante	7:00 P.M.
tú	dentista	8:00 P.M.
Tú y Verónica	parque	12.00 P.M.

12 ¿Cómo van a la escuela?

Look at the drawing and write how these people get to school every morning.

Yo voy en metro.

1. tú

____

2. Manuel

____

3. nosotros

____

4. Juanita y Ramona

____

5. José y Alejandra

____

6. el profesor

____

7. la profesora

____

8. tú y Marcela

____

Nombre: ______________________ Fecha: ______________

13 Una entrevista

As a journalist you are given the opportunity to interview a famous celebrity from Mexico (Luis Miguel, Selma Hayek, Ricardo Montalbán, etc.). Your boss gives you one hour to write at least eight questions for the interview. What would you ask? Search the Internet for the name of someone you might be interested in interviewing. Try to ask personal questions about what the person plans to do in the near future.

____

____

____

____

____

____

____

____

____

____

____

____

Nombre: ______________________________ Fecha: ______________

Lección 6

1 En la zona centro de México, D.F.

You have just returned from Mexico City and you are showing a friend some photographs you took during your trip. Identify what is shown in each photograph.

Es una avenida.

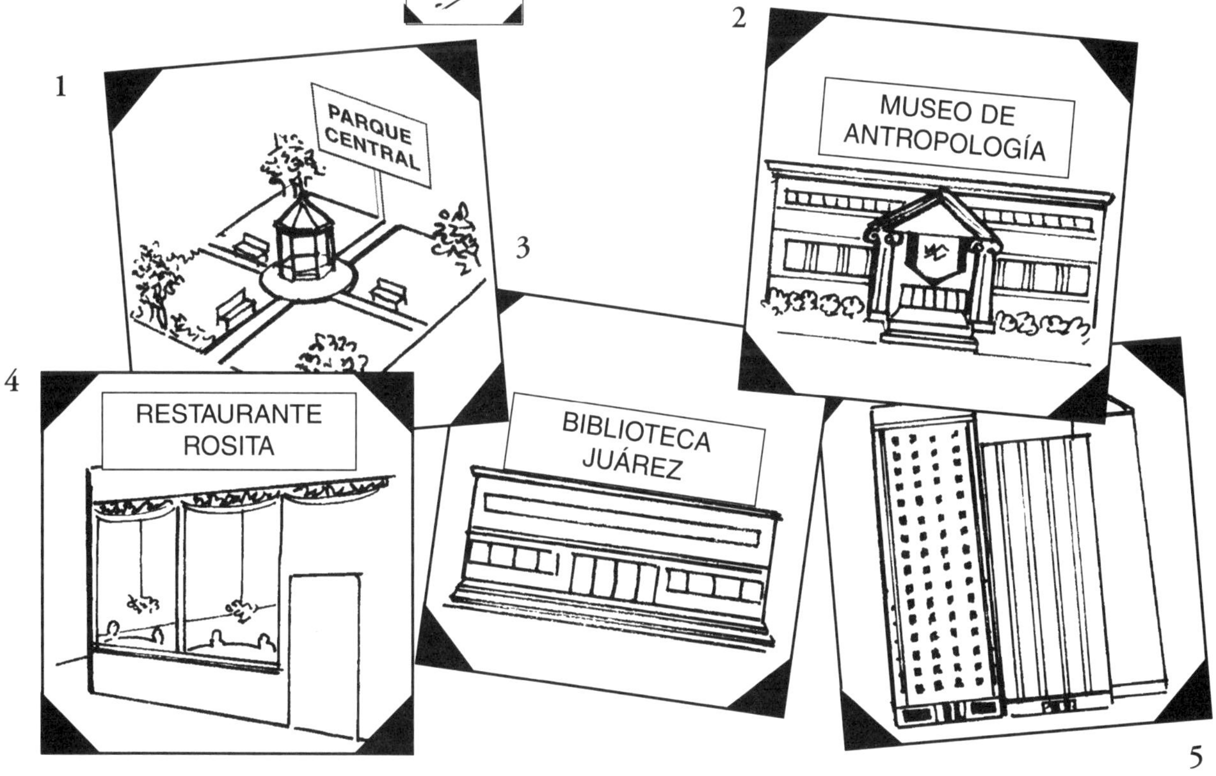

1. ______________________________

2. ______________________________

3. ______________________________

4. ______________________________

5. ______________________________

Nombre: ______________________________ Fecha: ______________

2 ¿Adónde van en la Ciudad de México?

As a tour guide in Mexico City, you need to confirm what everybody wants to do on their day off. Restate what each person will be doing at a given time and ask your assistant for confirmation.

Victoria/el Palacio de Bellas Artes/9:15 A.M.
Victoria va a ir al Palacio de Bellas Artes a las nueve y cuarto de la mañana, ¿verdad?

1. el profesor Bonilla/el Parque Chapultepec/3:00 P.M.

____

____

2. Lorenzo y Pepita/la Plaza de las Tres Culturas/1:00 P.M.

____

____

3. tú/el Museo de Antropología/10:00 A.M.

____

____

4. yo/el Teatro Orfeón/8:00 P.M.

____

____

5. Eva/el Monumento a la Independencia/12:30 P.M..

____

____

6. Elena/Coyoacán/2:45 P.M.

____

____

3 ¿Qué vamos a hacer?

Tell what the following people are going to do today according to the illustrations. Use the verbs from the list to write complete sentences in the space provided.

Ernesto
Ernesto va a ir al teatro.

ir	comer	caminar	hablar	necesitar

1. Carmen

____

2. Javier

____

3. Pedro

____

4. Esperanza y su amiga

____

5. Rodrigo

____

6. Marta

____

Nombre: ____________________ Fecha: ____________

4 La comida

Look at the following list of words related to food. As you read across the rows there are two things that belong and one that does not. Find the one that does not belong and circle it.

1.	frijoles	pescado	ver
2.	museo	ensalada	jugo
3.	agua mineral	teatro	refresco
4.	naranja	concierto	frijoles
5.	plaza	menú	mesero
6.	avenida	ensalada	pollo
7.	refresco	agua	saber
8.	pollo	pescado	menú

5 Sopa de letras

In the word-square find and circle ten items commonly found on a dinner table. The words may red forward, backward, horizontally, vertically or diagonally.

A	U	H	R	E	F	R	E	S	C	O
J	G	Z	X	A	L	W	G	R	O	W
Q	J	U	N	E	M	P	Q	A	M	M
B	M	N	A	R	A	N	J	A	I	O
Ú	N	E	M	M	M	S	U	G	D	R
Q	E	A	R	T	I	K	G	F	A	O
R	Q	R	U	T	R	N	O	Y	U	L
T	Q	E	Q	U	I	Q	E	M	C	L
M	H	S	E	L	O	J	I	R	F	O
I	H	E	N	S	A	L	A	D	A	P
T	M	M	O	G	I	O	A	K	L	L

6 Menú

At a restaurant in Mexico, one of your friends is having a difficult time deciding what to eat because every time he orders, you suggest an alternative dish.

Voy a comer frijoles.
¿Por qué no comes mole poblano?

1. Voy a comer ensalada de tomate.

   ____

   ____

2. Vamos a tomar agua mineral.

   ____

   ____

3. Voy a comer quesadillas.

   ____

   ____

4. Voy a comer tortillas y frijoles.

   ____

   ____

5. Voy a comer tacos de pollo.

   ____

   ____

6. Vamos a comer enchiladas.

   ____

   ____

7. Vamos a comer pescado.

   ____

   ____

Restaurante El Bocadito

ENSALADAS

Ensalada de tomate	N$10.00

PLATOS TÍPICOS

Arroz con pollo	N$21.00
Enchiladas	N$15.00
Mole poblano	N$27.00
Quesadillas	N$16.00
Tacos de pollo	N$17.50
Tamales	N$12.00
Frijoles	N$10.00
Tortillas	N$8.00

CARNES

Pollo frito	N$23.00
Pescado al horno	N$30.00

BEBIDAS

Jugo de naranja	N$8.00
Agua mineral	N$9.00

7 ¿Qué hacen?

Several activities are happening at your school today. Look at the drawings and use the appropriate form of *comer*, *comprender*, *leer* and *tomar* to write what the people below are doing.

Dolores
Dolores toma agua mineral.

1. Pepe

____

2. nosotros

____

3. Claudia

____

4. yo

____

5. Marcos y Mariana

____

6. Joaquín

____

7. Susana

____

8. Ignacio

____

9. Ramiro

____

Nombre: ______________________________ **Fecha:** ______________

8 En el restaurante

Manuela and Araceli are ordering food at their favorite restaurant, El Camino Real. Unscramble their dialog by numbering their statements in a logical order.

_______ ARACELI: Sí Muchas gracias, señor.

_______ MANUELA: Yo voy a tomar agua mineral.

_______ MESERO: Muchas gracias, señoritas.

_______ ARACELI: Pues, yo quiero pollo.

_______ MESERO: Muy bien. Van a comer pollo y pescado con ensalada y van a tomar agua mineral y un refresco. ¿De acuerdo?

_______ ARACELI: Y yo voy a tomar un refresco.

_______ MESERO: Buenas tardes, señoritas. ¿Qué van a tomar?

_______ MANUELA: Y yo voy a comer pescado con ensalada.

_______ MESERO: ¿Y qué van a comer?

9 ¡Vamos!

You and your friends want to do different things tonight. You are deciding what to do and looking at the newspaper's entertainment page. For each of your friend, suggestions you offer another. Follow the model.

¡Vamos a ver La Cenicienta!
¿Por qué no vamos a ver La Bella y la Bestia?

TEATRO

LA CENICIENTA
616-0511
Foro 11 de Escenaria
San Jerónimo 263, Pedregal de San Ángel
Dir. José Elías Moreno. Con Aylín Mujica.
Domingo, 11:30 hrs. $50

LA NOCHE DE LAS NARICES BIEN FRÍAS
593-8534
Teatro Wilberto Cantón
José María Velasco 59, San José Insurgentes
Dir. Rosa Chávez. Sábados y domingos,
11:30 y 13:30 hrs. Loc. $40

LA BELLA Y LA BESTIA
sistema ticketmaster 325-900
Teatro Orfeón
Luis Moya 40, Centro Histórico
Miércoles a viernes, 20:30; sábados 16:00 y 20:30;
domingo, 13:00 y 17:30 hrs.
Locs. $450, $250, $200, $170 y $90.
Para mayores de 4 años.

HACIENDO HISTORIA
702-2497
Museo de la Luz. Antiguo Templo de San Pedro
y San Pablo.
El Carmen esq. San Idelfonso, Centro
Un cocuyo y el fantasma de un jesuita
cuentan la historia del edificio del Museo de la Luz.

EL GATO CON BOTAS DE TIECK
55-9091 y 554-9099
Centro de Arte Dramático CADAC
Belisario Domínguez y Centenario, Coyoacán
Basado en un texto de Federico García Lorca.

1. ¡Vamos a ver "El Gato con Botas de Tieck"!

______

2. ¡Vamos al Teatro Orfeón!

______

3. ¡Vamos a las cinco y media!

______

4. ¡Vamos con Mariana y Marcos!

______

5. ¡Vamos al Centro de Arte Dramático!

______

6. ¡Vamos a ver "La Bella y la Bestia"!

______

7. ¡Vamos al Museo de la Luz!

______

8 ¡Vamos a ver "La noche de las narices bien frías"!

______

Nombre: ______________________ Fecha: ______________

10 La carta de Rosa

Rosa is on a school trip to Mexico City and she writes a letter to her friend, Alberto. Fill in the missing words with the correct forms of the verbs *hacer, ver, saber* and *comer*.

Hola Alberto:

¿Cómo estás? Yo estoy bien. Tú (1)______________ que estoy en la Ciudad de México, ¿no? Aquí (2)______________ mucha comida en los restaurantes y también (3)______________ mucho arte en los museos. Yo hablo español muy bien porque hablo con mis amigos y (4)______________ muchas preguntas. Tú (5)______________ español, ¿verdad? Los estudiantes aquí (6)______________ mucho inglés y también (7)______________ muchas preguntas. Guillermo y Nicolás (8)______________ muchos frijoles. No (9)______________ qué vamos a hacer mañana.

Tu amiga,

Rosa

11 Carta desde México

Imagine you are an exchange student living with a family in Mexico City. Write a letter to your parents describing your daily life. Include your favorite meals, places to visit and things to do.

____

____

____

____

____

____

____

____

Nombre: ______________________ Fecha: ______________

CAPÍTULO 4

Lección 7

1 Sopa de letras

In the word-square find and circle ten Spanish words for family members. The words may appear forward, backward, horizontally, vertically or diagonally.

L	A	W	F	O	I	Q	R	U	G	I
K	L	N	M	K	J	A	P	Q	Y	T
T	H	I	J	A	N	M	A	D	R	E
G	N	U	M	I	B	U	D	T	G	K
L	B	I	R	I	H	U	R	Q	T	Y
V	R	B	E	I	I	H	E	Q	Í	F
P	O	I	O	T	J	A	E	L	A	J
S	K	L	X	Í	O	M	A	M	A	G
G	R	E	O	O	P	O	H	I	J	H
A	M	I	R	P	J	A	O	I	H	N

2 La familia de Sofía

Complete the following paragraph about Sofía's family, using her family tree as a reference.

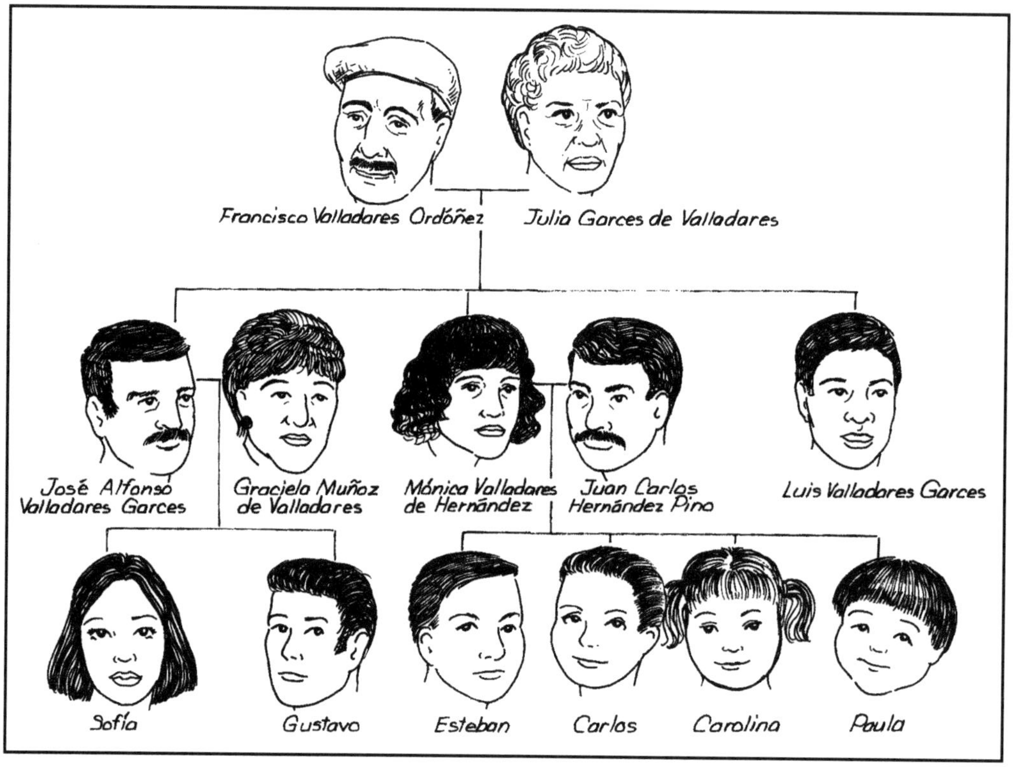

Hola, me llamo Sofía. Mi (1)______________ se llama Gustavo. Tengo cuatro (2)______________ que se llaman Esteban, Carlos, Carolina y Paula. Mi primo Esteban es muy simpático. Ellos son los (3)______________ de mis (4)______________ Mónica y Juan Carlos. Mi (5)______________ Mónica es la (6)______________de mi papá. Mi (7)______________ se llama José Alfonso y mi (8)______________ se llama Graciela. Tengo otro (9)______________, que se llama Luis. Él es muy divertido. Mis (10)______________ se llaman Francisco y Julia. Yo soy su (11)______________ favorita.

Nombre: ______________________________ Fecha: ______________

3 Carmen vive en Puerto Rico

Carmen is visiting you from Puerto Rico. She is showing you a map of the island and pointing out where she and her relatives live. Help her write complete sentences to say where she and her relatives live, using the clues given. Follow the model.

mi tía Julia/Bayamón
Mi tía Julia vive en Bayamón.

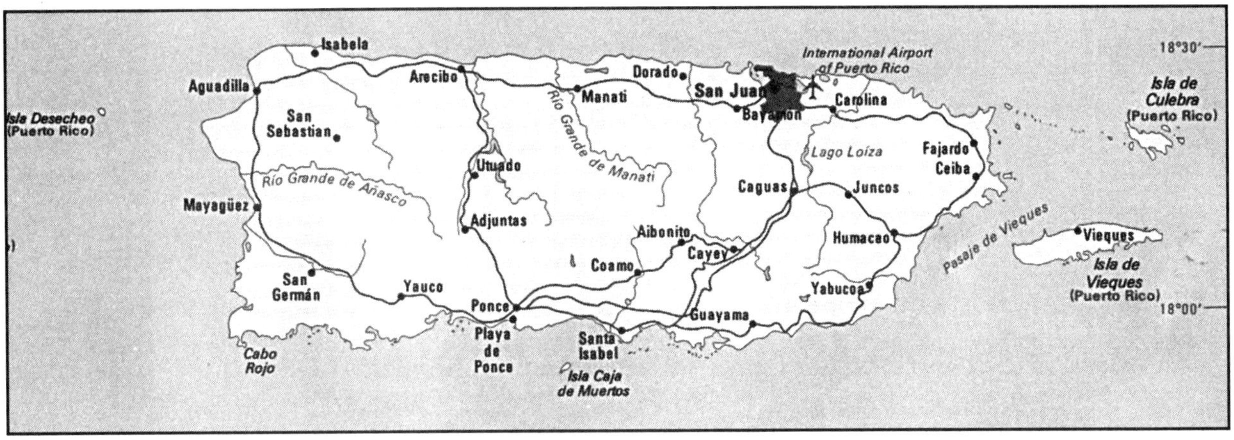

1. mi primo Gilberto/Aguadilla

____

2. mis tíos/Manatí

____

3. mis abuelos/San Juan

____

4. mi tío Raúl/Mayagüez

____

5. mi hermano Beto/Ponce

____

6. mi hermana Juana/Guayama

____

7. yo/Arecibo

____

4 Las actividades de Carmen

Carmen is telling you about life in Puerto Rico. Complete the dialog with the correct forms of the verbs *vivir* and *ir.*

CARMEN: ¡Hola!

TÚ: Hola, Carmen. ¿Cómo estás?

CARMEN: Estoy bien.

TÚ: Tú (1) ___________ en Puerto Rico con tu familia, ¿verdad?

CARMEN: Sí, pero (2) ___________ mucho a Miami para ver a mis amigos.

TÚ: ¿Dónde (3) ___________ en Puerto Rico?

CARMEN: Yo (4) ___________ en Arecibo.

TÚ: ¿Y tus hermanos (5) ___________ en Arecibo también?

CARMEN: No, mi hermano Beto vive en Ponce y mi hermana Juana (6) ___________ en Guayama.

TÚ: ¿(7) ___________ a Guayama para visitar a tu hermana?

CARMEN: Sí, (8) ___________ a visitar a mi hermana mucho.

TÚ: ¿Tu hermana (9) ___________ a Miami también?.

CARMEN: No, ella no va a Miami.

TÚ: ¿(10) ___________ a visitar a tus abuelos?

CARMEN: Sí, yo (11) ___________ a visitar a mis abuelos en San Juan. Ellos son muy amables y cariñosos.

TÚ: ¡Qué bueno! Y, ¿(12) ___________ mucho a la playa?

CARMEN: ¡Claro! Mis primas y yo (13) ___________ a la playa cerca de Arecibo.

TÚ: ¡Qué divertido!

5 Los adjetivos

Can you tell the difference between masculine and feminine adjectives and between those that are singular and plural? Circle the word in each row that does not have anything in common with the others.

1.	otro	muchos	cariñosos
2.	favoritas	cariñosas	fantásticos
3.	popular	otras	bonitas
4.	divertida	favorito	simpática
5.	amable	cariñoso	otros
6.	todas	populares	divertido
7.	simpática	fantástico	bonita
8.	otra	divertido	bonito

6 Te presento a mis amigos

Imagine that Humberto has invited you to a family party, and is telling you who the guests are. Complete the sentences with the correct form of the adjectives shown in parentheses.

Los chicos populares son mis primos. (popular)

1. La señora ______________ es mi tía. (amable)
2. La ______________ señora es mi abuela. (otro)
3. El chico ______________ se llama Antonio. (nuevo)
4. Él tiene ______________ hermanas. (mucho)
5. La chica ______________ es una de las hermanas de Antonio. (simpático)
6. Roberto y Andrés son mis sobrinos ______________. (favorito)
7. El señor ______________ es el amigo de mi tío. (divertido)
8. Mis amigos son muy______________. (divertido)

7 ¿Quiénes vienen a la fiesta?

Carmen is having a party next week and her mother is telling you who is coming? Complete the following phrases with *su* or *sus* to say who is coming to Carmen's party.

la tía Eulalia y sus hijas

1. doña Catalina y _______ sobrinos
2. el chico nuevo y _______ padres
3. Eduardo y _______ profesor
4. mis hermanas y _______ hijas
5. el señor González y _______ familia
6. las hermanas Girón y _______ tía
7. la señorita Nájera y _______ mamá
8. Marta y _______ amigas
9. Roberto y _______ hermanos
10. Víctor y _______ abuelos

8 Fotos de familia

Natalia is showing you photographs of her family and friends in Puerto Rico. Complete the dialog between you and Natalia with the appropriate possessive adjectives.

TÚ: Ellos son tus primos, ¿verdad?

NATALIA: Sí, ellos son (*1*)_____________ primos.

TÚ: Tu tía Yolanda es la tía de Carmen también, ¿verdad?

NATALIA: Sí, ella es (*2*)_____________ tía.

TÚ: ¿Es (*3*)_____________ hermano?

NATALIA: No, no es mi hermano. Es el hermano de Carmen.

TÚ: ¿Cómo se llama él?

NATALIA: (*4*)_____________ nombre es Beto.

TÚ: ¿Y quiénes son ellos?

NATALIA: Ellos son (*5*)_____________ amigos. Todos vamos al colegio San Luis.

TÚ: ¿Cómo se llaman (*6*)_____________ abuelos?

9 ¡A describir!

Imagine that your parents left you in charge of the house while they went away to visit your uncle. They call you to see how things are going. Based on the drawing, answer their questions.

1. ¿Cómo está tu hermana?

____

2. ¿Y cómo está tu hermano?

____

3. ¿Cómo está la abuela?

____

4. ¿Está limpia la casa?

____

5. ¿Está abierta la ventana?

____

6. ¿Y Campeón? ¿Cómo está?

____

7. Y tú, ¿cómo estás?

____

10 La llamada sorpresa

Susana surprises her friend Catalina with a phone call. Complete their telephone conversation with the appropriate forms of the verb *estar.*

CATALINA: Aló.

SUSANA: Soy Susana. ¿Cómo (1)_________ tú?

CATALINA: ¡Susana! Bien, gracias. ¿Y tú?

SUSANA: (2)_________ muy bien.

CATALINA: Oye, ¿dónde (3) _________?

SUSANA: (4)_________en Puerto Rico. Laura (5)_________ aquí también. Nosotras (6)_________ muy contentas.

CATALINA: ¿Y tus hermanos? ¿(7)_________ en Puerto Rico también?

SUSANA: No, ellos (8)_________ en Orlando, en casa de mis tíos.

CATALINA: ¿Cómo (9)_________ tus tíos?

SUSANA: Mi tía (10)_________ bien, pero mi tío (11)_________ enfermo.

CATALINA: Ay, lo siento.

11 ¿Cómo están?

Can you describe the following drawings? Complete the following sentences according to the illustrations with the appropriate form of the verb *estar.*

Las ventanas <u>están abiertas.</u>

1. La calle_________________.

2. La calle _________________.

Nombre: ______________________________ Fecha: ______________

3. Los chicos __________________.

4. La chica __________________.

5. Joselito __________________.

6. El profesor __________________.

7. El restaurante __________________.

8. Las bicicletas __________________.

12 ¡Qué divertido!

Match the situations on the left with appropriate expressions that you would use on the right. Write the letter of your answer choice in the space provided.

______ 1. A friend gives you a ride to the beach.
______ 2. The back seat of the car is full of garbage.
______ 3. You hear on the radio about software that translates English into Spanish.
______ 4. It is 99o Fahrenheit at the beach.
______ 5. The restaurant has the air conditioning set very high.
______ 6. Through the window you have a beautiful view of the sea.
______ 7. Your friend lost his dog in the park.
______ 8. Your friend decides to organize a field trip to Puerto Rico.

A. ¡Qué amable!
B. ¡Qué bonito!
C. ¡Qué caliente!
D. ¡Qué divertido!
E. ¡Qué fantástico!
F. ¡Qué frío!
G. ¡Qué sucio!
H. ¡Qué triste!

13 Estudiante de intercambio

Imagine you are an exchange student living with a family in Puerto Rico. Write a letter to your parents, describing your host family.

Nombre: ______________________ Fecha: ______________

Lección 8

1 Los amigos dominicanos

While on vacation in the Dominican Republic, you sit down to write a letter to your parents at home. Complete the letter with the words from the list.

alto amable chico dulce excelente inteligente morena simpática

Hola, mamá y papá:

¿Cómo están? Yo estoy bien. Me gusta mucho la República Dominicana.

Tengo dos nuevos amigos. Se llaman Rafael y Diana. Diana es (1)__________ y (2)__________. Rafael es (3)__________ y (4)__________. A ellos les gusta cantar y tocar la guitarra. Diana tiene una voz muy (5)__________ para cantar. Rafael toca la guitarra muy bien, es un músico (6)__________. También lee muchos libros de poemas. Él es un (7)__________ muy (8)__________.

2 La República Dominicana

Answer the following questions about the Dominican Republic.

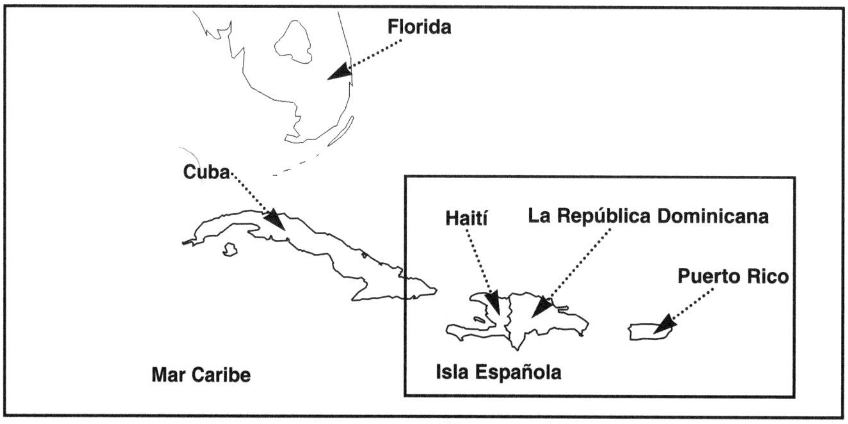

1. ¿Cómo se llama la música popular de allí?

____

2. ¿En qué océano está la isla La Española?

____

3. ¿Que países *(countries)* están en la isla?

____

4. ¿Cuál es la capital de la República Dominicana?

____

3 Me gusta bailar merengue

You have prepared a list of the things and activities that you like about the Dominican Republic. Complete the following sentences with either *me gusta* or *me gustan.*

1. __________ el merengue.
2. __________ las islas tropicales.
3. __________ ir a la playa de Boca Chica.
4. __________ jugar al béisbol.
5. __________ las chicas inteligentes.
6. __________ la música del Caribe.

4 ¿Qué te gusta?

Imagine that your new friends, Rafael and Diana, ask you many questions about your pastimes and interests. Answer their questions with complete sentences.

¿Te gusta hablar español?
Sí, (No, no) me gusta mucho hablar español.

1. ¿Te gusta comer pescado?
____
2. ¿Te gustan los conciertos de rock?
____
3. ¿Te gustan los museos?
____
4. ¿Te gustan los partidos de béisbol?
____

5 Nos gusta

Write five complete sentences in Spanish, using any of the expressions from the box to say what you and your family like or dislike doing.

Nos gusta ir a las playas.
No nos gusta mirar fotos.

mirar fotos · leer libro · *jugar al béisbol* · ir de compras · **ver la televisión** · las fiestas · **ir a conciertos** · *oír la radio*

1. ______________________________
2. ______________________________
3. ______________________________
4. ______________________________
5. ______________________________

6 Me gusta oír música

Study these profiles of teenagers in the Dominican Republic who are looking for pen pals in the United States. Then answer the questions that follow, according to the information in the profiles.

Nombre: Marisol Guerra
Dirección: Avenida Rómulo Betancourt #673
Edad: 15
Pasatiempos: bailar música tropical, ir al cine, jugar al béisbol, ver la televisión

Nombre: Gabriel Pérez
Dirección: Avenida Las Palmas #123
Edad: 18
Pasatiempos: salir con los amigos, bailar, ir a la playa

Nombre: Elena Jiménez
Dirección: Avenida 27 de Febrero y calle Dr. Fernando
Edad: 13
Pasatiempos: tocar música, bailar, leer, oír la radio

Nombre: Tomás Alarcón
Dirección: Las Mercedes #134
Edad: 15
Pasatiempos: jugar béisbol, salir con los amigos, leer revistas, ver la televisión

Nombre: Rosa Vargas
Dirección: Paseo Pte. Billini #289
Edad: 16
Pasatiempos: jugar al béisbol, leer libros, ir de compras, ver la televisión

Nombre: Mario Trujillo
Dirección: El Conde y Santomé
Edad: 17
Pasatiempos: cantar, ir a la playa, ver la televisión

1. A Mario y a Gabriel, ¿les gusta ir a la playa?

____

2. ¿Le gusta jugar al béisbol a Elena?

____

3. ¿A quiénes les gusta ver la televisión?

____

4. ¿A quién le gusta tocar música?

____

5. ¿Qué le gusta hacer a Rosa?

____

6. ¿A quiénes les gusta bailar?

____

7. ¿A quiénes les gusta leer?

____

8. ¿A ti qué te gusta hacer?

____

7 ¿A quién le gusta?

Look at the following drawings of several people and the things they enjoy doing. Write complete sentences to describe what each likes to do, using prepositional pronouns for emphasis.

A él le gusta hablar.

1

2

3

4

5

6

7

8

1. ______________________________
2. ______________________________
3. ______________________________
4. ______________________________
5. ______________________________
6. ______________________________
7. ______________________________
8. ______________________________

Nombre: ______________________ Fecha: ______________

8 Sopa de letras

In the word-square find and circle twelve words used to describe a person. The words may read forward, backward, horizontally, vertically or diagonally.

I	E	G	O	Í	S	T	A	O	I	P	C
R	N	A	I	V	G	U	D	H	B	T	A
O	M	T	N	P	E	A	L	T	A	R	C
I	C	E	E	E	G	O	R	O	J	S	Ó
B	O	M	C	L	R	O	B	L	O	I	M
U	Z	T	E	I	I	H	R	P	D	A	I
R	A	D	Y	R	E	G	O	D	M	L	C
U	B	O	A	R	O	N	E	R	O	M	O
C	A	L	V	O	O	E	R	N	L	P	D
G	N	E	S	J	D	A	I	G	T	B	V
M	I	S	B	O	S	O	R	E	N	E	G

9 ¡Qué interesante!

Choose the situation or situations where you might use each expression.

1. As soon as you board the airplane, you fall asleep. You wake up just as the plane lands in the Dominican Republic.
2. You are watching a women's basketball game on TV and see a player dunk the ball.
3. You go to a museum and learn what the conquistadores did to the original inhabitants of La Española.
4. At the museum you learn about all the different people and cultures that have influenced modern culture in the Dominican Republic.
5. You go to a restaurant and order a local dish.
6. You miss your return flight and must spend ten hours in the airport waiting for the next one.

¡Qué horrible! ____________________

¡Qué aburrido! ____________________

¡Qué alta! ____________________

¡Qué rápido! ____________________

¡Qué bueno! ____________________

¡Qué interesante! ____________________

10 ¿Cómo son?

Write a description of each picture in the space provided. Follow the model.

Alfonso
Alfonso es bajo.

1. el profesor Ricardo Maldonado

______

2. Gloria

______

3. Julio

______

4. la profesora Teresa Álvarez

______

5. Juan

______

6. Ana

______

7. Pablo

______

11 ¿Dónde es la fiesta?

Consuelo and Aníbal are talking about a party. Complete their conversation with the correct forms of *ser* and *estar*.

CONSUELO: ¡Hola! ¿Cómo (1) __________?

ANÍBAL: (2) __________ bien, ¿y tú?

CONSUELO: Muy bien, gracias.

ANÍBAL: ¡Qué bonita (3)__________hoy!

CONSUELO: Gracias. Voy a una fiesta de Beneficio.

ANÍBAL: ¿Dónde (4)__________ la fiesta?

CONSUELO: (5) __________en el Hotel Excelsior.

ANÍBAL: ¿Con quién vas?

CONSUELO: Voy con Graciela.

ANÍBAL: ¿Quién (6)__________ ella?

CONSUELO: (7)__________la amiga de mi prima. Ella (8)__________ en nuestra clase de historia. (9)__________ alta, morena y muy bonita.

ANÍBAL: Ah, sí. Ella nunca (10) __________triste, ¿verdad?

CONSUELO: Sí, ella (11)__________ muy divertida.

12 Entrevista con una persona famosa

Surprise! Juan Luis Guerra is at the same benefit concert you are attending. His public relations person allows you to ask him eight questions. What would you ask him? Begin by asking how he is, what he likes or does not like, and so on. Write your questions in Spanish in the space provided.

1. ______________________
2. ______________________
3. ______________________
4. ______________________
5. ______________________
6. ______________________
7. ______________________
8. ______________________

CAPÍTULO 5

Lección 9

1 Sopa de letras

In the word-square find and circle nine items related to music. The words may read forward, backward, horizontally, vertically or diagonally.

M	G	R	A	B	A	D	O	R	A	J
E	A	J	N	S	C	T	S	E	A	U
R	E	R	C	I	A	Z	Z	N	D	O
E	S	S	I	D	O	L	Ó	A	R	C
N	T	O	C	A	D	I	S	C	O	S
G	É	B	Z	G	C	O	T	A	J	I
U	R	Z	T	N	A	H	L	Z	M	D
E	E	R	A	R	G	E	I	A	S	E
J	O	C	A	S	E	T	E	R	A	M
A	M	A	R	R	A	T	I	U	G	U

2 ¡Qué país!

While visiting Costa Rica, you discover many exotic new things to see and do. Write the expression that best fits each situation using *qué* plus a noun.

You go to a fantastic national park.
¡Qué parque!

1. From the top of a tall building you have a beautiful view of San José.

____

2. You watch a very interesting movie about a rare species of unusual golden-colored frogs.

____

3. You go to a marvelous new song concert.

____

4. You run into your next-door neighbor from the United States, who is also visiting Costa Rica.

____

3 ¿Qué tienen en la maleta?

What do these people have as they prepare to leave on a trip to Costa Rica? Complete the following sentences with the appropriate form of the verb *tener*.

Cristina *tiene* un cuaderno.

1. Nosotros ____________ dos libros sobre Costa Rica.

2. Cristina y Ángel ____________ cuatro discos compactos de Inti Illimani.

3. Andrés ____________ una guitarra.

4. Nosotros ____________ muchos casetes de salsa.

5. Yo ____________una grabadora.

6. Inés ____________ mucho dinero.

7. Tú ____________ fotos de Costa Rica.

8. Ramón____________ un mapa de San José.

Nombre: ______________________ Fecha: ______________

4 ¿Qué tienen en las manos?

You are part of a tour group in Costa Rica and your flight from San José to Puerto Limón has been delayed. Look at the following illustration and write what each person has to help pass the time at the airport.

Hugo tiene un periódico.

1. Cristina ______________________.

2. Ramón ______________________.

3. Inés y la profesora Sabati ______________________.

4. Inés ______________________.

5. Ángel y yo______________________.

6. Yo______________________.

7. César______________________.

5 ¿Te gusta la música?

Ramón interviewed two Costa Rican students during the trip. Help him complete a written transcript of the interview by filling in the blanks with the appropriate forms of *tener* and *gustar.*

RAMÓN: ¿Cuántos años (1) __________, Gilberto?

GILBERTO: (2)__________ quince años.

RAMÓN: ¿Y tú, Antonio, cuantos años (3)__________?

ANTONIO: (4)__________quince años también.

RAMÓN: ¡Qué sorpresa! Uds. dos (5) __________ quince años.

GILBERTO: Sí, también (6)__________ quince clases.

RAMÓN: ¿Te (7) __________ la música salsa?

ANTONIO: Sí, me (8)__________ mucho.

GILBERTO: A mí también me gusta.

RAMÓN: Gilberto, ¿(9)__________ discos de Rubén Blades?

GILBERTO: Sí, (10) __________discos compactos y cinco casetes.

ANTONIO: Yo también los tengo y me (11)__________ir a sus conciertos cuando (12)__________ dinero.

RAMÓN: Gracias por la información, muchachos.

6 ¿Lo tienes?

Your mother is checking to see if you have the following items in your suitcase before leaving on your trip to Costa Rica. Complete the answers to her questions by using *lo* or *la* as needed.

1. ¿Tienes la grabadora?

   Sí, __________ tengo.

2. ¿Tienes el dinero?

   No, no __________ tengo.

3. ¿Tienes el casete?

   Sí, __________ tengo.

4. ¿Tienes la maleta?

   Sí, __________ tengo.

5. ¿Tienes la música de Silvio Rodriguez?

   No, no __________ tengo.

6. ¿Tienes el disco compacto de la nueva canción?

   Sí, __________ tengo.

7. ¿Tienes la guitarra?

   No, no __________ tengo.

8. ¿Tienes la revista de música?

   Sí, __________ tengo.

7 Lo veo

Look at the drawing of a classroom and write whether or not you see the following objects.

¿Ves el mapa de Costa Rica?
Sí, lo veo.
¿Ves la guitarra?
No, no la veo.

1. ¿Ves el teléfono?

____

2. ¿Ves la revista?

____

3. ¿Ves la playa?

____

4. ¿Ves el libro de historia de Costa Rica?

____

5. ¿Ves la computadora?

____

6. ¿Ves el disco compacto?

____

7. ¿Ves la grabadora?

____

8. ¿Ves el dinero?

____

8 Las necesito

Your friends have many questions for you. Answer their questions using the appropriate direct-object pronouns.

¿Haces un viaje a Costa Rica?
Sí, (No, no) lo hago.

1. ¿Compras las canciones de Selena?

____

2. ¿Tienes fotos de tu viaje?

____

3. ¿Buscas los casetes de música para bailar?

____

4. ¿Lees los periódicos de Costa Rica?

____

5. ¿Hablas español?

____

6. ¿Necesitas dinero?

____

7. ¿Comes tamales?

____

8. ¿Cantas canciones de la nueva canción?

____

9 Un mensaje musical

Look at the following advertisement for cassettes, albums and compact disks. Then answer the questions, using the personal *a* when appropriate.

1. ¿Te gusta escuchar música?

2. ¿Te gustan los casetes o los discoscompactos?

3. ¿Qué tipo de música escuchas?

4. ¿Escuchas a Camilo Sesto?

5. ¿Escuchas a Ana Gabriel?

6. ¿Escuchas a Juan Luis Guerra?

7. ¿A quién escuchas más?

8. ¿A cuál de estos cantantes ves en la televisión?

9. ¿Cuál de estos casetes vas a comprar?

10. ¿A qué cantante te gustaría *(would like)* escribir? ¿Por qué?

10 Crucigrama

Complete the following crossword puzzle.

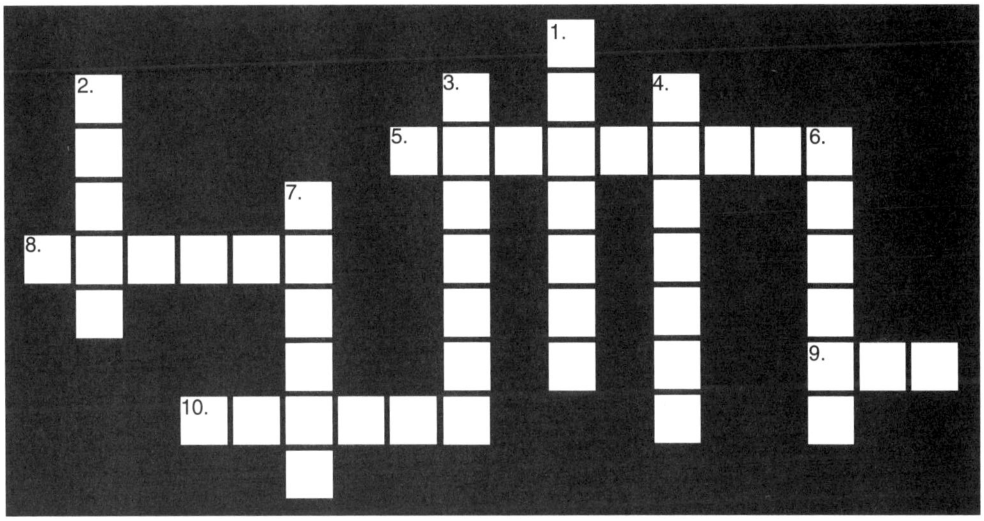

Horizontales

5. Hoy es jueves; ayer fue _.
8. La _ tiene siete días.
9. El _ tiene 24 horas.
10. Hoy es miércoles; mañana es_.

Verticales

1. Para saber a qué hora son tus actividades necesitas un _.
2. Hoy es domingo; mañana es _.
3. Hoy es jueves mañana es_.
4. La escuela está cerrada el _.
6. Hoy es viernes; mañana es _.

11 El calendario de Ernesto

You just have entered Ernesto's personal Web page by accident. Look at Ernesto's calendar and answer the following questions.

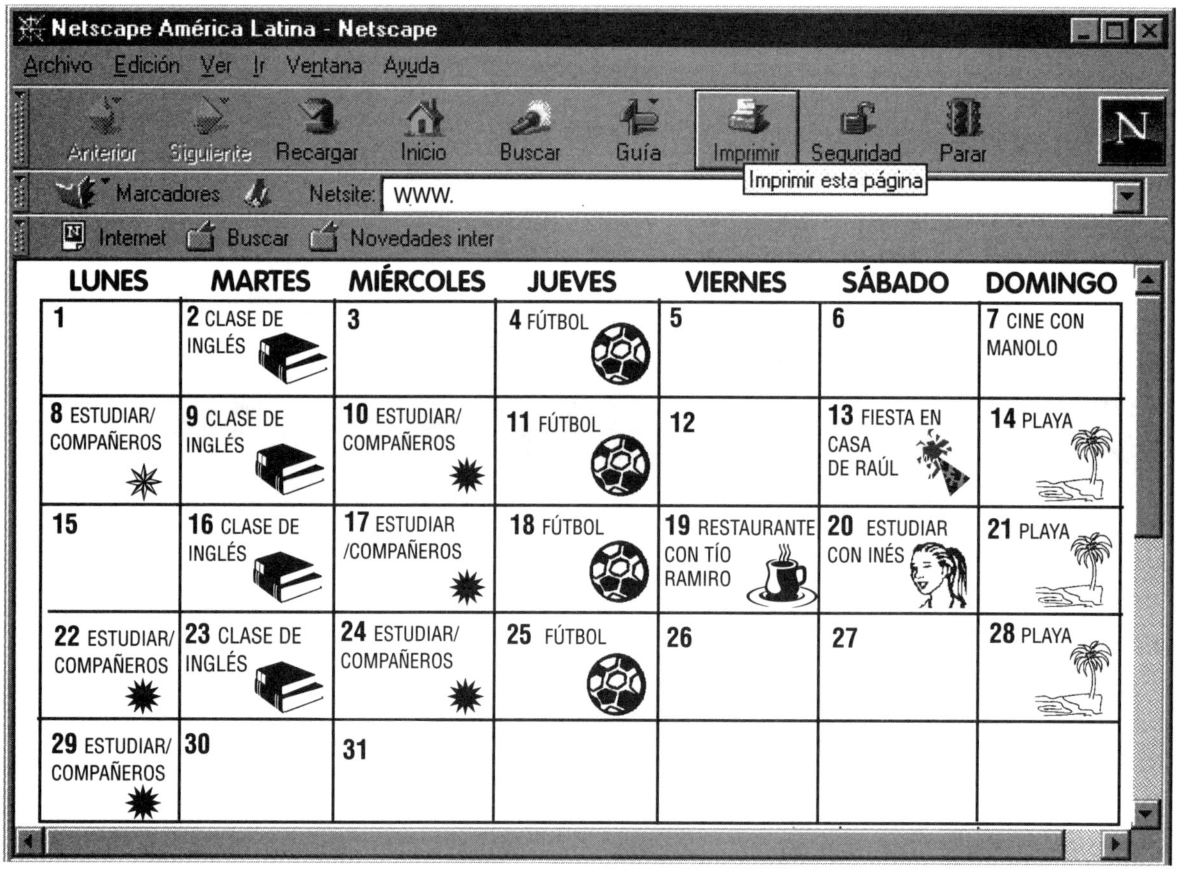

LUNES	MARTES	MIÉRCOLES	JUEVES	VIERNES	SÁBADO	DOMINGO
1	2 CLASE DE INGLÉS	3	4 FÚTBOL	5	6	7 CINE CON MANOLO
8 ESTUDIAR/ COMPAÑEROS	9 CLASE DE INGLÉS	10 ESTUDIAR/ COMPAÑEROS	11 FÚTBOL	12	13 FIESTA EN CASA DE RAÚL	14 PLAYA
15	16 CLASE DE INGLÉS	17 ESTUDIAR /COMPAÑEROS	18 FÚTBOL	19 RESTAURANTE CON TÍO RAMIRO	20 ESTUDIAR CON INÉS	21 PLAYA
22 ESTUDIAR/ COMPAÑEROS	23 CLASE DE INGLÉS	24 ESTUDIAR/ COMPAÑEROS	25 FÚTBOL	26	27	28 PLAYA
29 ESTUDIAR/ COMPAÑEROS	30	31				

1. Hoy es domingo7. ¿Dónde está Ernesto?

____

2. ¿Qué días va Ernesto a la playa?

____

3. ¿Qué días va a jugar al fútbol?

____

4. ¿Cuándo es la fiesta en casa de Raúl?

____

5. ¿Qué hace Ernesto los martes?

____

6. ¿Qué va a hacer el viernes 19?

____

7. ¿Cuándo va a estudiar con Inés?

____

8. Qué hace Ernesto los lunes y los miércoles?

____

12 ¿Qué planes tienen?

What do these people have planned for this week? Combine elements from each column to write eight sentences.

el lunes	mi hermano/a	llamar a un amigo
el martes	tú	ir a caminar por la playa
el miércoles	mi profesora	mirar televisión
el jueves	Uds.	hacer un viaje
el viernes	nosotros	estudiar español
el sábado	mis amigos	tocar el piano
el domingo	yo	ir a montar en bicicleta
la semana que viene	doña Elena	comprar discos compactos

1. ____
2. ____
3. ____
4. ____
5. ____
6. ____
7. ____
8. ____

13 Una excursión fantástica

In one or two paragraphs, describe the things you will do each day of the week during a visit to Costa Rica. Also, mention the things you will not do and explain why.

Nombre: ______________________ Fecha: ______________

Lección 10

1 La carta de Isabel

Isabel wrote Remedios the following letter. Fill in the space provided with a word that best completes the sentence.

Managua, jueves 29 de octubre

(1) _______________ Remedios:

¿Cómo estás? Yo estoy bien. Ayer (2)_______________ mi cumpleaños. Mañana, (3)_______________ , voy a tener una fiesta para (4)_______________ mi cumpleaños en casa de mis tíos en León. ¡Va a ser una fiesta (5)_______________! Mis primos y mis amigos van a estar allí todo el fin de semana. El (6)_______________ vamos a ir a la playa y el (7)_______________ vamos a ir a comer en un restaurante. Estoy muy triste porque no vas a (8)_______________a mi fiesta de cumpleaños en León. Pero sí, vas a venir pronto ¿verdad?

Tu (10)_______________ de siempre,

Isabel

Nombre: ______________________ Fecha: ______________

2 El amigo de Nicaragua

Daniel, your pen pal from Nicaragua, has been writing to you about places in his country. Locate them on the map and write the name of each place in the space provided.

Lago de Managua	Managua	Costa de los Mosquitos	Lago de Nicaragua
Río Tipitapa	Costa Rica	Océano Atlántico	Océano Pacífico

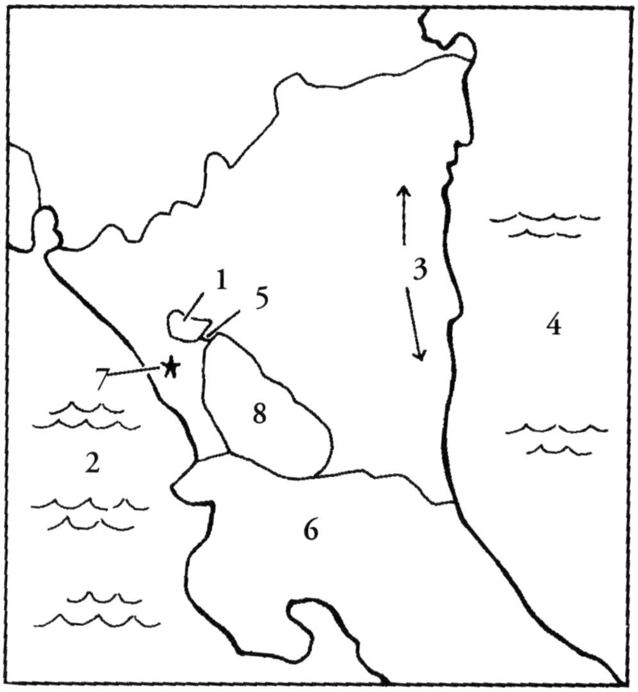

1. ______________________
2. ______________________
3. ______________________
4. ______________________
5. ______________________
6. ______________________
7. ______________________
8. ______________________

3 ¿De donde vienen a la fiesta?

Juan Carlos is celebrating his birthday and has invited friends and family from several countries to his birthday party. Match the letter of the country with the information in the numbered list.

A. Vienen de México.
B. Viene de Guatemala.
C. Vienes de la República Dominicana.
D. Viene de la Argentina.
E. Viene de Honduras.
F. Viene de México.
G. Viene de Costa Rica.
H. Viene de los Estados Unidos.

______ 1. Ana/Buenos Aires
______ 2. la abuela de Juan Carlos/Los Ángeles
______ 3. la tía/Tegucigalpa
______ 4. los primos/Monterrey
______ 5. Paola/Antigua
______ 6. yo/Santo Domingo
______ 7. Javier/Acapulco
______ 8. Cristina/San José

4 ¿Cómo vienen?

Look at the drawings and write complete sentences to tell how these people are arriving to Juan Carlos' party. Follow the model.

Vinicio
Vinicio viene a la fiesta en barco.

1 

2 

3 

4 

5 

6 

7 

8 

1. Ana
____
2. los primos
____
3. el tío José Arcadio
____
4. Aureliano
____
5. Cristina y Paloma
____
6. la tía Antonia
____
7. Lalo Contreras
____
8. Javier y Galo
____

Nombre: ______________________________ Fecha: ______________

5 Los Verdes en concierto

Carlos and Luis are in the school cafeteria talking about a benefit concert for the ecology club. Complete their conversation with the words from the list.

viernes
día
pasado mañana
el cumpleaños
la semana
cuándo
anteayer
los martes

CARLOS: ¡Oye! ¿Qué (1) ____________________ es hoy?

LUIS: (2)____________________ . ¿Por qué?

CARLOS: Hoy es el concierto de Los Verdes.

LUIS: No, el concierto fue (3) ____________________ .

CARLOS: ¿Y qué tal?

LUIS: ¡Fantástico! Hay otro concierto (4) ______________ que viene. ¿Vas a ir?

CARLOS: ¿(5)____________________ es?

LUIS: El martes.

CARLOS: No, porque todos (6) ____________________ tengo clase de guitarra.

LUIS: Mira, (7)____________________ tengo una fiesta en mi casa. ¿Vienes?

CARLOS: ¡Qué lástima, Es (8) ____________________ de mi abuelo. Lo siento, chico.

Nombre: ______________________ Fecha: ______________

6 ¿Qué día fue?

Use the calandar below to complete the following sentences.

Si hoy es jueves ocho, *pasado mañana* es sábado diez.

LUNES	MARTES	MIÉRCOLES	JUEVES	VIERNES	SÁBADO	DOMINGO
			1	2	3	4
5	6	7	8	9	10	11
12	13	14	15	16	17	18
19	20	21	22	23	24	25
26	27	28	29	30	31	

1. Si hoy es martes veinte, ______________ fue domingo dieciocho.
2. Si ayer ______________ miércoles veintiocho,
   ______________ es viernes treinta.
3. Si anteayer fue jueves veintidós, ______________ es lunes veintiséis.
4. Si ______________ es méircoles catorce,
   ______________ es viernes dieciséis.
5. Si ______________ fue viernes dos,
   ______________ fue jueves primero.
6. Si ______________ es sábado veinticuatro hoy es viernes veintitrés.
7. Si ______________ es miércoles siete,
   ______________ fue martes seis.
8. Si ______________ es domingo dieciocho,
   ______________ fue jueves quince.

Nombre: ______________________________ Fecha: ________________

7 Encuentra los meses

In the word-square find and circle the twelve months of the year. The words may read forward backward, horizontally, vertically or diagonally.

A	P	A	G	O	S	T	O	I	F	N
S	B	S	B	P	R	Z	E	A	E	S
E	L	R	M	K	R	X	N	G	B	T
P	H	I	I	A	I	M	O	O	R	E
T	N	U	M	L	Y	U	V	W	E	N
I	B	J	U	N	I	O	I	T	R	E
E	R	U	E	I	I	B	E	O	O	R
M	G	L	O	T	E	A	M	L	I	O
B	D	I	C	I	E	M	B	R	E	R
R	R	O	C	T	U	B	R	E	J	E
E	J	E	I	Q	W	Q	E	E	T	Q

8 Los días de fiesta

How well do you know the months and the major holidays that take place in those months? Match the names of holidays on the right with the dates on the left. Write the letter of the holiday in the space provided.

______ 1. Es el 25 de diciembre.

______ 2. Es el 4 de julio.

______ 3. Es el primero de mayo.

______ 4. Es el 6 de enero.

______ 5. Es el 28 de diciembre.

______ 6. Es el primero de enero.

______ 7. Es el 31 de diciembre.

______ 8. Es el 14 de febrero.

A. el Día de San Valentín
B. el Día de los Inocentes
C. la Navidad
D. el Día del Trabajo
E. la Noche Vieja
F. el Día de los Reyes Magos
G. el Año Nuevo
H. el Día de la Independencia de los Estados Unidos

Nombre: ______________________________ Fecha: ____________

9 La lista de fechas de Andrea Catalina

Andrea Catalina had trouble remembering the birthdays of relatives and friends, but now she has made a list with their names and dates of birth. Based on Andrea Catalina's list, answer the following questions with complete sentences.

¿Cuándo es el cumpleaños de Sebastián?
Es el 3 de octubre.

Nombre:	Fecha de nacimiento:
Manolo	26 de noviembre de 1985
Soledad	8 de marzo de 1983
Ana Macarena	14 de febrero de 1978
el abuelo Rafael	17 de septiembre de 1920
la tía Julia	5 de julio de 1950
Sebastián	3 de octubre de 1990
Gabriela	28 de septiembre de 1987

1. ¿Cuántos años tiene Sebastián?

____

2. ¿Cuándo cumple años Gabriela?

____

3. ¿Cuántos años tiene el abuelo Rafael?

____

4. ¿En qué mes es el cumpleaños de la tía Julia?

____

5. ¿Cuántos años tiene Ana Macarena?

____

6. ¿Cuándo es el cumpleaños de Soledad?

____

7. ¿Cuántos años tiene Soledad?

____

8. ¿En qué día y en qué mes es el cumpleaños de Manolo?

____

Nombre: ______________________ Fecha: ______________

10 ¿Cuánto te gusta?

Look at the list of celebrations and write one of the following expressions with gustar to express how much you like or dislike the celebrations below.

me gusta · no me gusta ni un poco · me gusta mucho · no me gusta · me gusta un poco

1. celebrar mi cumpleaños

____

2. celebrar el cumpleaños de mi hermano

____

3. celebrar la Navidad

____

4. celebrar el Año Nuevo

____

5. celebrar el último (*last*) día de clases

____

6. celebrar el Día de la Independencia

____

7. celebrar el Día de San Valentín

____

8. celebrar el Día de la Madre

____

11 Los precios de ahora

Look at this newspaper advertisement for items on sale and answer the following questions. Spell out the numbers in your answers.

¿Cuánto cuesta *(cost)* el carrito para verduras?
Cuesta mil seiscientos sesenta y siete.

1. ¿Cuánto cuesta la olla de presión?

____

2. ¿Cuánto cuesta el juego de café para cuatro personas?

____

3. ¿Cuánto cuesta la cafetera?

____

4. ¿Cuánto cuestan las vajillas?

____

5. ¿Cuánto cuesta la silla plegable?

____

6. ¿Cuánto cuesta el juego de café para seis personas?

____

7. ¿Cuánto cuesta la hielera plástica para bar?

____

Nombre: ______________________ Fecha: ______________

12 Los días de la Independencia

When did Latin American countries gain independence from Spain? Write the dates of independence for the following countries.

Nicaragua: 15/9/1821
el quince de septiembre de mil ochocientos veintiuno

1. Ecuador: 24/5/1822

____

2. República Dominicana: 27/2/1844

____

3. Argentina: 9/7/1816

____

4. Colombia: 20/7/1810

____

5. Guatemala: 15/9/1821

____

6. Venezuela: 5/7/1811

____

7. México: 16/9/1810

____

8. Chile: 18/9/1810

____

Nombre: ______________________ Fecha: ______________

13 Correo electrónico

Write an e-mail to a friend telling him or her how old you are, when your birthday is and what you plan to do to celebrate it. Include the name of the people that are coming to your celebration.

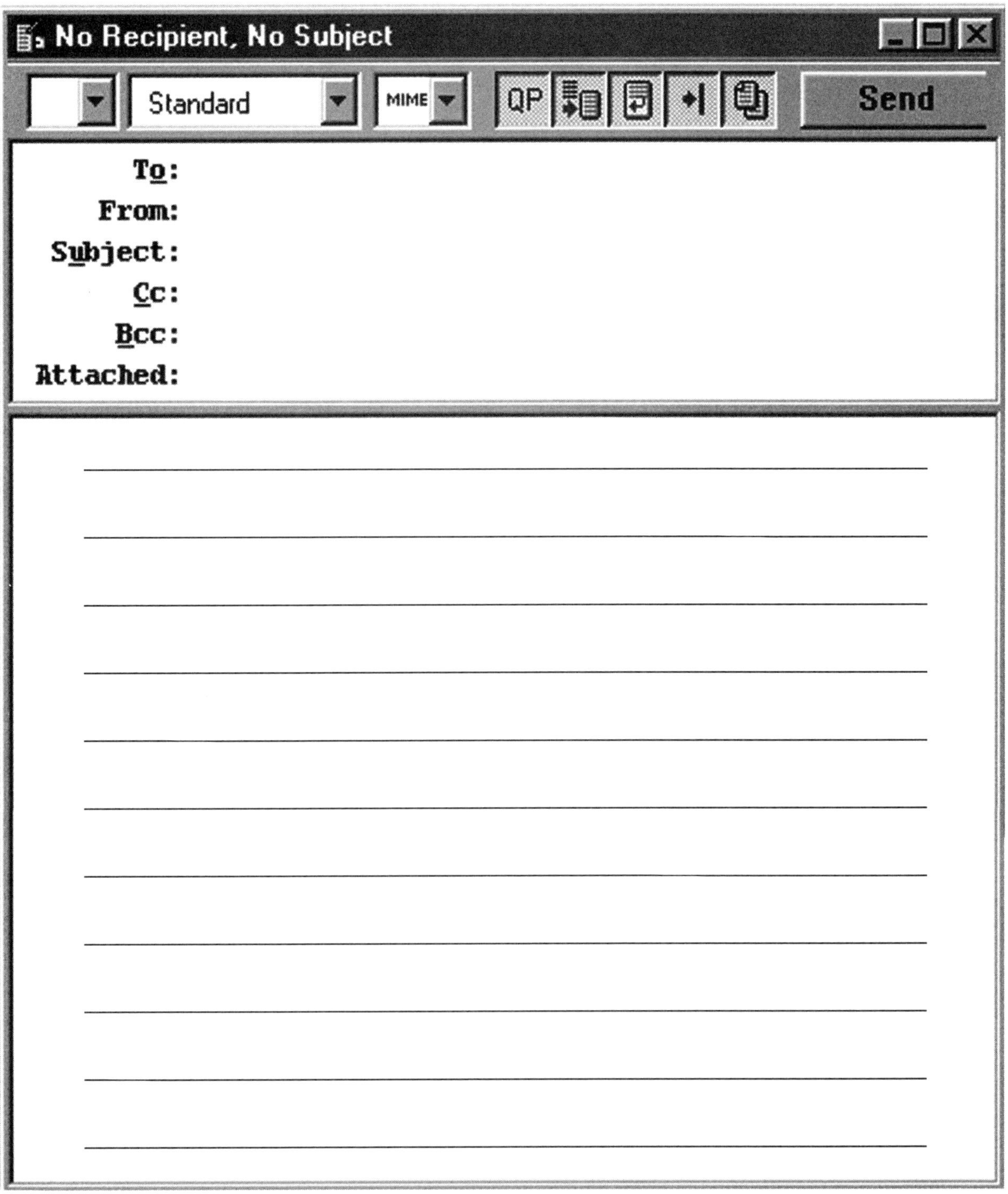